*Heaven Bound in a Hollywood World*
By Frieda Dowler

"This book has really changed the way I allow society to put enormous pressure on me today. By allowing God to take the lead, I have been able to see the things he wants for me and quiet down all the voices that tell me 'I'm not good enough, rich enough, or pretty enough'. This book has truly changed my life and made me so incredibly thankful for my unique walk in this world." Brooke–age 20

"I feel like you wrote this just for me." Haedon–age 21

"It will push you to know yourself better." Cindy–age 55

"This book could be for anyone." Mary–age 82

"What a complete explanation for young women to understand her struggles and see the big picture of why it is so hard to stay on course. I think if they keep it up for 33 days it will definitely change lives." Ruth Hostetler, MS–Therapist and Educator, Southside Pastoral Counseling

"This book speaks to the heart of a group that often slips through the cracks of the local church, the 20-somthings. Dowler's transparency and authenticity creates an encouraging and safe literary environment allowing her to present challenging truths and connect with her readers. My prayer is that as young women work through this book, they will grow in Christ and in self." Rachael Long–Director of Family Ministries, Emmanuel Church

"I have worked with children, youth, and young adults in medicine and psychiatry for over 30 years. I can say the need for this book is great. It makes the young adult look into herself, find hope, direction, and purpose in future and begin to look outside themselves to a greater world vision based on eternal life." Patti Rubino MSN-CNS, RN, PNP, Child/Adolescent Psychiatric Nurse Practitioner.

# HEAVEN BOUND
## IN A **HOLLYWOOD** WORLD

FRIEDA DOWLER

# HEAVEN BOUND
# IN A HOLLYWOOD WORLD

*33 Days to Change Your World*

*Heaven Bound in a Hollywood World*
Copyright © 2015 by Frieda Dowler. All rights reserved.

No part of this publication may be reproduced, stored in a retrieval system or transmitted in any way by any means, electronic, mechanical, photocopy, recording or otherwise without the prior permission of the author except as provided by USA copyright law.

This book is designed to provide accurate and authoritative information with regard to the subject matter covered. This information is given with the understanding that the author is not engaged in rendering legal, professional advice. Since the details of your situation are fact dependent, you should additionally seek the services of a competent professional.

Published by Frieda Dowler

*Author photo by Gwen Edwards*
*Interior design by Angelo Moralde*
*Cover design by Larry P. Taylor*

Published in the United States of America
ISBN: 978-0-692-97536-7

1. Self-Help / Spiritual
2. Religion / Christian Life / Spiritual Growth
15.03.19

# CONTENTS

Introduction ............................................................. 10
Prologue ................................................................. 12

## Challenge 1

Change Your Reality ..................................................... 15
Day 1 Your Journey Begins: From Hollywood to Heaven ..................... 17
Day 2 Wait a Minute, Isn't Heaven for Later? ............................ 23
Day 3 Breaking Out of a Hollywood Mentality ............................. 28
Day 4 Whose World Is It? ................................................ 32
Day 5 A Friend in High Places ........................................... 37
Day 6 Citizens of Two Worlds ............................................ 42
Day 7 A New Heart for a New Start ....................................... 48
Day 8 Enter Your New Reality ............................................ 54

## Challenge 2

Change Your Identity .................................................... 63
Day 9 A New You ......................................................... 65
Day 10 Skinside: Your Body .............................................. 69
Day 11 Skinside: Hollywood Says ......................................... 73
Day 12 Skinside: Heaven Says ............................................ 77
Day 13 Your Skinside .................................................... 85
Day 14 Inside: Your Soul ................................................ 88

Day 15 Inside: Hollywood Says . . . . . . . . . . . . . . . . . . . . . . . . . . . . . . . . . . . . . 93
Day 16 Inside: Heaven Says . . . . . . . . . . . . . . . . . . . . . . . . . . . . . . . . . . . . . . 98
Day 17 Your Inside . . . . . . . . . . . . . . . . . . . . . . . . . . . . . . . . . . . . . . . . . . . . 102
Day 18 Deeperside: The Spirit . . . . . . . . . . . . . . . . . . . . . . . . . . . . . . . . . . . 106
Day 19 Deeperside: Hollywood Says . . . . . . . . . . . . . . . . . . . . . . . . . . . . . . 110
Day 20 Deeperside: Heaven Says . . . . . . . . . . . . . . . . . . . . . . . . . . . . . . . . . 114
Day 21 Your Deeperside . . . . . . . . . . . . . . . . . . . . . . . . . . . . . . . . . . . . . . . 120
Day 22 Otherside: Our Serving Side . . . . . . . . . . . . . . . . . . . . . . . . . . . . . . 125
Day 23 Otherside: Hollywood Says . . . . . . . . . . . . . . . . . . . . . . . . . . . . . . . 128
Day 24 Otherside: Heaven Says . . . . . . . . . . . . . . . . . . . . . . . . . . . . . . . . . 132
Day 25 Your Otherside . . . . . . . . . . . . . . . . . . . . . . . . . . . . . . . . . . . . . . . . 136

## Challenge 3

Change Your Community . . . . . . . . . . . . . . . . . . . . . . . . . . . . . . . . . . . . . . 139
Day 26 Why Community? . . . . . . . . . . . . . . . . . . . . . . . . . . . . . . . . . . . . . 141
Day 27 Who Is My Community? . . . . . . . . . . . . . . . . . . . . . . . . . . . . . . . . 145
Day 28 Heaven's Community . . . . . . . . . . . . . . . . . . . . . . . . . . . . . . . . . . 152
Day 29 Maintaining Your New Reality . . . . . . . . . . . . . . . . . . . . . . . . . . . 157
Day 30 Warning: Beware of Identity Theft . . . . . . . . . . . . . . . . . . . . . . . . 160

## Challenge 4

Change Your Story . . . . . . . . . . . . . . . . . . . . . . . . . . . . . . . . . . . . . . . . . . . 167
Day 31 Past . . . . . . . . . . . . . . . . . . . . . . . . . . . . . . . . . . . . . . . . . . . . . . . . . 169
Day 32 Present . . . . . . . . . . . . . . . . . . . . . . . . . . . . . . . . . . . . . . . . . . . . . . 171
Day 33 Future . . . . . . . . . . . . . . . . . . . . . . . . . . . . . . . . . . . . . . . . . . . . . . 174

# INTRODUCTION

Do famous personalities determine your reality? Media celebrities, athletes, rock stars? Do you identify with a particular brand? Do you feel like you have to measure up because of the pressure of those around you?

Do expectations from society, the media, and even those you love create the reality you live in? What if you could change that reality? What if you could get a new view of it? What if you could remove the pressure of appearance, achievement, and performance?

You can. But it starts with being honest and true, being uniquely you, being the one God created.

But how can we know who we are when we don't take the time to figure it out? We are constantly listening to the messages we get from the media, messages from Hollywood, and messages from others silently telling us who we should be.

At one time, the standard of Christianity was the biggest influence on behavior. Those standards created a line in the sand to know what was acceptable and what was not. Even though many crossed the line, they knew where the line was. But those lines have been crossed and justified so many times that the lines have become blurred. Christianity's never changing standards have been replaced with Hollywood's ever changing standards. Now there is no aim or goal for societal behavior and it's adding to the confusion about who we should be.

So, what basis do we use to live life? People try different roles, hoping to find one they're sure of. They post on Facebook, delete Facebook, then post a different personality. With standards that keep changing, we are never sure of who we are and how we should act.

Wouldn't it be great to have a book that tells us how to live our lives, how to discover who we are, and how to live with purpose? One that considers our individuality yet guides our choices?

What if that book is the Bible? Would we want to know what it has to say? Would we take the time to discover our identity according to God? Would we trust God, who made us in His image and for a purpose on the earth? Could we learn to know and love God, accept ourselves, and influence others in order to make the world a better place?

This four-part book is designed to help you answer those questions. Commit to 30 minutes a day for the next 33 days, and it will change your world.

- "Challenge 1: Change Your Reality" explores your beliefs. It challenges you to begin this journey by believing in heaven. Starting with the end in mind is the key to success in any venture.
- "Challenge 2: Change Your Identity" shows how to view yourself as three distinct parts—body, soul, and spirit. By understanding the differences, you can learn to accept yourself and develop a goal of influencing the world through God's love.
- "Challenge 3: Change Your Community" explains why it's important to develop relationships with others who understand these goals and our purpose as Christians.
- "Challenge 4: Change Your Story" asks you to journal your plan of commitment, determination, and hopes.

Your destiny of heaven is at risk. The challenge before you is to be proactive—to act in advance—not simply wait until the end to find out where you will spend eternity. This will give you aim and purpose for life. This book doesn't come with images that are instantly transferred into your head, like the media. It will take time and thought to form you, the person God has made, then to realize your purpose in the world. It is a journey into the inside, to the deepest part of your soul and spirit.

# PROLOGUE

**What follows is a personal story that started my journey to discovering a meaningful life.**

I stood in the doorway, choking back tears. Spatters of bright red blood on the floor and walls of a light blue and white-tiled bathroom nauseated me. The brilliant fluorescent lighting captured the image like a flash photo in my mind. The blood was the evidence of an attempted suicide by one of my college friends. Paramedics had wheeled her to the waiting ambulance, eight floors below, leaving us behind staring at the gruesome site. The residence advisor left with her in the ambulance and left us to sort our emotions together…and to clean the mess.

After tearful hugs and questions, I mustered the courage to go into the bathroom where she had used a razor blade to deeply slice her wrists, severing arteries and even tendons. My overriding sense of responsibility kicked in as I realized fresh blood would be easier to clean than dried blood.

The others stood in the hall passing towels from the linen closet. I wetted them in the sink and quickly made the first swipe. The blobs of blood had already begun to dry around the edges while the centers swiped across the tiles and sucked into the grout. This was more than I imagined. I took a deep breath, blinked away the tears as I pushed aside my own pain and scrubbed harder.

"More towels," I said as I ran them under the water from the faucet, leaving them a little wetter. I passed them back to the girls in the hall.

"What should we do with the bloody towels? Should we wash them?"

"No, I don't think we should keep them. Just throw them into a trash bag and take them to the dumpster. No reminders."

As if any of us would ever forget.

My mind flashed back to one year ago when I was the one taking a ride in the ambulance. My roommate had successfully interrupted my suicide attempt. She came in before there was blood. An emotional breakdown followed. I was near the end of my first college semester and I pulled it together enough to finish my finals. After that, I moved home to heal.

During this emotional healing, I realized I had given up control of my life to someone. Who was this guy that he could have that kind of power over me? My destiny did not belong to him. It belonged to me. I had given myself to him and my sense of duty told me I must stay in this rela-tionship despite his manipulative personality. A phone call from a friend telling me he had been cheating caused mixed feelings. I had convinced myself that I belonged to him, no matter how he treated me. He, on the other hand, felt the freedom to stray. Angry at myself for being so naive, I couldn't come up with a way out of the relationship except trying to end my life. It was a brief unplanned moment, interrupted at the right time. I thank God He had another plan for my life.

In the years that followed, I completely disregarded my Christian upbringing, believing I could manage my own life. I built walls to protect myself from anyone controlling my life. My college friend's suicide attempt a year later, also over a boyfriend, emphasized that for me. I took the atti-tude of "love 'em and leave 'em". No one would ever own my soul again. I became very independent, moving a thousand miles from home and memories, to finish college. I continued to work in that same city for another couple of years after graduation, being a carefree young professional. "No strings attached" was my motto for every relationship. But in the process, I became very unhappy and lacked purpose for my life. I had built a bubble that no one could penetrate. Before long, I felt isolated and unable to love. I felt dead inside.

It took me four years to realize that I could not even successfully control my own life. That responsi-bility was too big and I had made a mess of it. I needed help. That's when God reached into my world. I began to see and hear things I had not considered before. Like how God was real and how He heard me when I pray. They were things about a spiritual life—a life on the inside of me. I decided to allow God, through the guidance of the Holy Spirit, to show me that way of life. I joined other people who understood this path, and my spirit life began to grow. I read my Bible to hear from God, and talked to Him as I prayed. I never looked back but kept going forward in this new life.

That was in the 1970s, but it is relevant today. The Bible tells us there is nothing new under the sun, even though it might look a little different. The schemes of God's enemy, Satan, are always the same—to keep us from loving God, from loving ourselves, and from loving others. But when we discover how to do that, we will live life with meaning and purpose, a rewarding life.

My goal in writing *Heaven Bound in a Hollywood World* is that you come to know God in a per-sonal way. Let Him be the center of your world. We all need someone besides ourselves. He offers guidance in a world of chaos. This is an interactive journey, containing quotes, diagrams, quizzes, and journaling because reading, writing, and speaking aloud are ways to confirm the principles you will learn. My hope is you will continue to visit this book in years to come, to remind yourself of who you are, where you are going, who your enemy is and to update your status.

King David of the Bible said the following:

All the days ordained for me were written in your book before one of them came to be. How precious to me are your thoughts, O God! (Ps. 139:16b–17a, niv)

Oh, let me rise in the morning and live always with you! (Ps. 139:118b, msg) Believe the same is true for each on this journey.

# CHALLENGE 1

## Change Your Reality

Day 1

## Your Journey Begins: From Hollywood to Heaven

At some point in life, crisis occurs. Emotionally stressful or traumatic events cause us to go in a different direction when the unexpected happens. My crisis happened when I was in college and trust was broken in what I thought was a serious relationship. I reached a turning point and decided not to trust anyone again because the pain was too much to bear. I believed I could only trust myself.

Four years later, I reached another crisis. I had become hardened and questioned whether I would ever be able to love again. I knew staying isolated was not the answer but I was afraid to risk feeling deep pain again. This time I decided to trust God. I saw how others who were living in relationship with God were experiencing joy. That was missing in my life. I was twenty-three when I entered into a relationship with God. I had learned about God when I was young, but I had never known God personally. He has been there through every difficult situation I have faced. He has never broken my trust. And the promise of being with Him forever is heaven, where there will never be pain or sorrow. We will have troubles on earth but trusting God and having faith in heaven gives hope.

I had a shift in my reality. I was living a Hollywood reality and chasing my dreams. I was after external and temporary things. I wanted career, money, things, status, and of course, love. Hollywood teaches self-fulfillment is the key to success and happiness. That kind of reality never satisfies. It is a vicious cycle of striving and disappointment, keeping us hungry for more.

But there is another reality—the one Jesus came to show. He came from God's kingdom and He taught about its reality while He walked the earth. That's the reality on our inside. It is the reality of our thought life because that is what motivates our actions. His words made such an impact that He revolutionized the way people lived. He taught it's what's in our hearts that matters. He taught we should be motivated by love for Him and for others, not just love for ourselves. He taught

God's ways, the standards in the kingdom of heaven. When we have a heart to please God then our behavior will follow.

## Hollywood's Reality

Appearance, achievement, and recognition are what Hollywood's reality is based on. But its standards are on a sliding scale. What's acceptable depends on who's the most influential at the moment, whether in our circle or in the media. Standards of behavior continually change, causing confusion. Trying to keep up with those changes is exhausting and leads to breakdowns.

Findings suggest almost one fourth of the people in the US are being treated for some sort of mental disorder. I believe brain science exploration is partially the reason for these statistics, but humanity's exposure to expectations from a mixture of sources is causing the average person turmoil. Ranging from mild to severe, and just to mention a few, these mental disorders include: mood disorders, eating disorders, schizophrenia, bipolar disorder, anxiety disorder, panic disorder, obsessive/compulsive disorder, social phobias, and attention deficit hyperactivity disorder; all say we need help. Grant it, brain chemistry can get out of whack, but so can emotions throwing us into confusion and acting it out.

This sliding scale of standards is causing many to develop their own standards. They set rules about what's acceptable and hope God understands their needs. They become the center of the universe. You at the center implies everything will revolve around your standards. Everyone must meet your expectation. What you say is right. What you say goes. If it doesn't meet your expectation, then it's wrong. And that gives you the right to be critical or unhappy with others.

In this kind of reality, no one gets along with each other for very long. You won't find anyone who will agree with you 100 percent. It brings arguments and a breakdown in relationships. You will either dominate others, or you will be dominated by other's expectations. Dominating others will lead to isolation and loneliness. If you allow others to dominate, you will never be able to develop into the person you were meant to be.

For others, reality is based on what the body experiences through the five senses: touch, sight, smell, taste, and sound. Hollywood promotes an endless supply of visual stimulants for our senses creating desire. It is intoxicating. We keep going for more. Until one day, we realize those stimulants don't satisfy for very long. Then we need another stimulant. We are driven to pursue other pleasures. In most cases, those stimulants lead to heartbreak, pain, or addiction.

Inside all of us is a longing for peace but Hollywood's yo-yo standards won't permit it. Keeping up with what's expected and chasing after personal satisfaction causes continual striving. Eventually, it leads to a breakdown. But if it weren't for that breakdown, many would not try to find a solution. Many would not try to find God. If we could be God and create our own balance and harmony, we would never need a change. It's the pain that leads us to find another way.

We need a different center for our world. We need God's standards, which never change, to be the center. And we need something besides pursuing the pleasures of our five senses and trying to satisfy ourselves. We need something besides pursuing self-fulfillment. We need a sixth sense to keep focused on what's really important in this world. Heaven's reality is the change we need.

*Based on the above, which fits you most?*

- *Striving to please others*
- *Striving to please yourself*

*In Heaven's reality, we only need to please one – that is God.*
*Malachi 3:6a NLT says, "I am the Lord and I do not change".*
*There is comfort in things that don't change. They are reliable and will always produce the same results. Knowing God never changes, implies I must be the one to change if I want different results in my life.*
*Prayer: God help me change my reality. Help me learn to please you only.*
*(Write your own prayer)*

_____
_____
_____

## Heaven's Reality

First, you must decide you *want* what's good for you. Do you want a new reality? Do you want peace? If you do, it will require some action on your part. To begin with, you must resist the message of Hollywood. It will be difficult because it permeates society. The underlying message of Hollywood is "me first" which is basic human nature. You can learn to resist that urge by replacing it with "God first." Putting God at the center of every decision will lead to a rewarding life both now and forever.

But we, as a society, are addicted to Hollywood. It captures our senses with glitzy, glamorous images of a make believe reality. Have you ever noticed how easy it is to do the thing that isn't good for us? It's easy to obtain. Like junk food or _____, (you fill in the blank). Who doesn't want Taco Bell over broccoli? Choosing the best for us takes effort. (You can't get broccoli at a drive-thru, you have go to the store, bring it home, and cook it.) But science confirms it is better for us. And in our mind, we know it's true. But in our passivity, we choose Taco Bell.

To do what is good for us takes putting our mind on it and then making ourselves do it. Like the teachings of Jesus, action follows thought. So the thought process comes first. Sometimes before we start a new action, we need to stop, resist, or abstain from something that is not good for us. Sometimes that is the most difficult part. But you've heard the saying "You are what you eat". That not only applies to our bodies but it applies to our minds; you become what you feed your mind.

When deciding to change your reality, you must first consider the results of your present reality. Then consider if you changed your reality, what different results you expect to get. If you are totally satisfied with your present reality, you can stop reading now. You don't need what's in this book. But if you are like a majority, we need help. Something has to change. I suggest changing your perception of the way things seem in the world today. There is a different reality than Hollywood presents. It is the reality of heaven. We can't see heaven because it has been overshadowed by Hollywood. (Kind of like broccoli—it doesn't stand out on the street with a neon sign, it's hiding in the produce section at the grocery. You have to go and find it.)

The world of Hollywood is doing a great job entertaining. We have 24-hour access and it's everywhere we turn. We have become a society that craves entertainment. But it's diverting our attention from the things that are important. The things of heaven don't entertain, they train. It takes effort to train but it takes zero effort to be entertained. The result of being continually entertained is that it takes away initiative. Training increases energy and determination toward a task. Do nothing and the standards and ideals of Hollywood is your reality. Decide to learn and train yourself to think God's way and heaven can be your reality.

Over the next thirty-three days, be intentional about the things you read. Take the time to develop a new reality. Learn to view the world through the lens of God's standards. These things have helped me and I can navigate my circumstances because I have a new reality. I hope they help you, too.

> *Jesus told us when he lived on earth that the Kingdom of Heaven is about developing Godly character on the inside of us. In order to do so we must first transform our thinking process. The Hollywood culture screams in our ears and its visual images flash before our eyes causing it to dominate our senses, driving our thinking process. The message of the Kingdom of Heaven does not hunt us down, we must pursue it. It is a whisper in this noisy world. Since God is love, he does not force His thinking on us. In learning to love God, we must begin to understand his ways. It requires time away from this noisy world. This is the beginning of learning to know God and to trust His ways more than your own.*
>
> *Plan a place where you can get away on a regular basis to talk to God. Make it a special place where you will want to spend time. Make it secret, make it secluded, make it pretty, and make it comfortable. Where will you make your place to meet with God?*
>
> "He who dwells in the secret place of the Most High
> shall abide under the shadow of the Almighty."
>
> Psalm 91: 1 NKJ

> *I believe I need a change in my reality. I commit the next 33 days to learning what it takes to develop a new viewpoint. Each day I will go to my "special place" to read, meditate, pray, and journal (without interruptions from my phone). If I miss a day, I will continue the following day, believing it will help me reshape my reality. No one is watching me, except God. This is a commitment I make to myself and no one else. In doing so, I expect to learn how to be Heaven Bound in a Hollywood World.*
>
> Signed: _____
> Date: _____

Day 2

## Wait a Minute, Isn't Heaven for Later?

We've all heard about heaven. Most people believe in heaven but when asked to define or describe it they are usually vague. We simply believe it exists based on traditions, myths, and the hope that someday all our pain and suffering will cease because life is hard. And really, there has to be something besides this life, right?

All religions believe in an afterlife of some sort. Usually, it's based on a reward system and if we're good enough we will go there when we die. Some religions believe we get more than one chance to try to make it to heaven. But the place of heaven is a generally accepted as something in the afterlife.

I learned a lot about heaven as a child. My parents took me to church every Sunday morning and evening. Not only that, they took me to prayer meetings on Wednesday evenings. Heaven was talked about a lot. It was always the goal when you died and the preacher frequently reminded us we never knew when that would be so we better be ready. What I learned about heaven stuck with me. It was always my hope after death.

But I began drifting from church. As soon as I was old enough, I started working, and my schedule included Sundays and most Wednesdays. As I entered high school, very few friends went to church. I wanted to be accepted by them so subconsciously I compromised my attitude about being ready for heaven at any moment. Gradually, my desire to please my friends began to replace my desire to please God. I began to assume the attitude that God would understand, because after I had my fun, I would return to following Him. After all, I was young and there would be plenty of time later for the God stuff.

## Abbey's Story

How many of us put God on hold while we have our fun? Abbey's story shows how most of us feel:

Abbey turned seven yesterday and was hopeful about a couple of things that were coming up. Her parents had planned a trip to visit her cousin who lived near Disney World. They would experience the Magic Kingdom together. Soon after the trip, she would start second grade with her favorite teacher from kindergarten who had transferred. Abbey had missed her terribly during the first grade.

But today was Sunday, five days from their trip, and her family was on the way to church. Dad hummed to the Christian radio station adding a few words as he knew them. Mom finished her makeup in the rear view mirror, mascara, and then lipstick. Baby brother happily sucked his binky while Abbey daydreamed about wearing a Cinderella costume.

Upon arriving at church, Abbey asked Mom's permission to go to the Sunday school room by herself since she was now seven. Mom was confident she would be okay because they were among trusting people. Abbey certainly knew the way. They had attended this church since she was three.

Inside the classroom, Abbey happily greeted her friends, playing and talking until the teacher said it was time to start the lesson. The teacher began with a prayer. She said the word heaven and Abbey's thoughts went to Disney World. She wondered if Disney World would be better than heaven because it was made for kids. Oh, what fun she was going to have.

After the prayer, the teacher asked the children, "Who wants to go to heaven?" Everyone except Abbey raised their hand. This puzzled the teacher but she didn't want to embarrass Abbey by questioning her in front of the others. The teacher continued with a story from the Bible and ended with the memory verse for the week:

> There are many homes up there where my Father lives, and I am going to prepare them for your coming. When everything is ready, then I will come and get you, so that you can always be with me where I am.
>
> —John 14:2–3a, NIV

At the end of class, the teacher handed each of the children an index card with the memory verse written on it. If they memorized it by next Sunday, they would earn a treat. Abbey loved the teacher's treats but knew she would miss next Sunday because of their trip. The teacher sensed Abbey's reluctance when she handed her the card.

After dismissing the children, the teacher politely asked Abbey to stay behind for a minute. "Abbey, I don't understand why you don't want to go to heaven. Would you please tell me?" Abbey's eyes moved from the teacher to the floor. "I do want to go to heaven, just now right now. I want to go to Disney World first and I want to be in my favorite teacher's class when school starts."

The teacher understood. Abbey thought she was talking about right now and Abbey had plans for her future that she didn't want to give up.

## Live Like Heaven Is Now

Abbey is exactly like many of us. Heaven can wait. We have plans. How many of us delay the decision to follow God, afraid it will require giving up our plans?

We can't imagine God's plans are better than ours. Has he watched TV or been to the latest movie? How about the travel channel and those exotic beaches? And what about plans for vacations, husbands, homes, children and careers? Not to mention iPhones, tablets, other widgets and gadgets we want? What about those, God? Can we have all that and still have heaven?

The question for most, like Abbey, is do we want heaven now? Jesus's message was about the kingdom of heaven, named 40 times in the Bible and the kingdom of God, named 91 times. The Bible does tell of a future place where we will be with God in the afterlife and Jesus told us what it would be like. He would know. He came from there. But He also told us we should look for that kingdom now, on earth, within ourselves. He said it like this when the leaders of his day questioned Him about heaven, God's kingdom.

> One day the Pharisees asked Jesus, "When will the kingdom of God begin?" Jesus replied, "The kingdom of God isn't ushered in with visible signs. You won't be able to say, "It has begun here in this place or there in that part of the country." For the kingdom of God is within you.
>
> —Luke 17:20–21 TLB

What if the now heaven, the one inside, became our reality? What if it could become a light, or a central focus, guiding us in decisions leading us to the eventual place of forever heaven? Would we want that? I don't know about you, but with all the choices I face daily, I need help. I need a plan and a basis for making decisions. Random decisions get random results and I want to live a rewarding life now and forever.

## Change Your Reality by Answering the Question

Abbey didn't realize she could raise her hand in response to the teacher's question, "Who wants to go to heaven?" Abbey was conflicted. She wanted to go to heaven but she wanted her desires fulfilled. So it is with us. We all have dreams about life and yes, sometimes Hollywood prompts those dreams. Are we willing to include heaven when it comes to fulfilling our plans?

Most have heard the message of heaven. How God, Jesus, the Holy Spirit and the Bible help lead us there. It stirs controversy because it is a personal message. Many have tried to interpret their personal message as a message for the masses. It has caused arguments, and even wars, over the centuries. But the personal message gets to the core of each individual; who we are, what we believe, and how we live.

In talking to His disciples, Jesus described four kinds of soil in a parable. The simple story illustrates four kinds of people who hear God's message. Read the story and decide which kind of soil you are. Each person must eventually respond to the question of heaven's reality. How will you respond?

**Get Personal**
Read: Mark 4: 1–20 The Parable of the Four Soils

Journal:

- Which soil are you?
  _____
  _____
  _____

- Do you have plans for heaven?
  _____
  _____
  _____

- What plans are more important to you than heaven?
  _____
  _____
  _____

- How has this influenced your thinking?
  _____
  _____

*Prayer: God, I want be good soil. I ask you to help make me receptive to your words so they can produce good results in my life.*

*(Write your own prayer.)*
_____
_____
_____

Day 3

# Breaking Out of a Hollywood Mentality

## Believe Heaven's Story

The Bible is referred to as "the good book" but it's more than that. It is the story of humankind, both historically and spiritually. It contains truth, inspired of God. It is the story of separation from God, His love for humankind, and how to be in a close relationship with God. It contains promises for now and later.

When the Bible is read just as a book, it will tell of the circumstances of the times—basically a historical account of the Israelites, past and future. But when the Bible is read for guidance, it becomes miraculous. It becomes personal when our hearts are truly seeking God's guidance. The Holy Spirit, God's spirit, interprets it to each individual no matter what our circumstances may be. It is a book passed from generation to generation for a reason. It remains the best seller ever because it is a love letter written to millions of hearts. Reading the Bible regularly and allowing God's Holy Spirit to guide you personally is the key step to staying heaven bound in a Hollywood world.

The Bible may seem overwhelming or confusing. It's so big and you may think history is boring but it's important to know the overview of the Bible. It helps to put everything in perspective. Below is a story that explains the overview in fairy tale form. The Bible has a plot which is the main theme, but it's easy to lose that plot when there are other subplots going on, like all through the Old Testament. It's also easy to misunderstand the Bible when we only take the pieces we like. It all goes together for a reason. It will bring understanding to life when taken in its entirety. This is this story of separation, love, and reconciliation for the Israelites, known as God's chosen people, as well as all of humanity, and each of us individually.

## The Plot

There was a king who owned everything. He had children who lived abundantly in his kingdom. They happily did what they could to increase the abundance of his kingdom. In return, he provided everything for them. He told them everything he had belonged to them. He only asked one thing of them. He asked them not to eat from one tree because it was poison. They would die if they ate the fruit of it and become separated from him and the kingdom. This would serve as the evidence of the children's continuing love for their king and it came with fatal consequences.

A villain quietly invaded the kingdom. He told the children they would not die if they ate the fruit of the tree. Instead, their wisdom would increase, and like him, they would be wiser than the king. At that moment, the children removed their eyes from the king's love. They questioned the truth and believed the villain's lies. They ate from the tree. When this happened, instantly the children became separated from the king to seek their own wisdom. The villain stole their hearts so they went with the villain to his kingdom.

They didn't have the life the villain promised. He didn't provide everything for them. He made them work, providing everything for themselves and he kept them in captivity. The villain told them this was how they would increase their wisdom, by their own effort. It was a hard life—full of pain, suffering, and mistrust. The children soon forgot how good they had it.

Their lives became drudgery. They were slaves to the villain, doing his will. If they became dissatisfied, the villain would allow them to experience something good. But the pleasure was only temporary. It always led back to being his slave.

This vicious cycle kept repeating itself until the king devised a way to bring his children home. He entered their world in disguise, became one of them, and told them how much he missed them and that he forgave them. He was with them for a while, telling about life in the kingdom they had forgotten. Created deep in their soul was a desire for the beautiful life they could have.

Some ignored him but many believed it was the king in spite of his disguise. They listened to what he said as he told them he would eventually destroy the villain's world. They could return to his beautiful kingdom forever. But the opposite happened. The villain captured the king and had him killed. It looked as if he had been defeated. This crushed the hopes of his children.

Then a miracle happened. The king came to life. This happened in order to prove to his children he was more powerful, honest, and trustworthy than the villain. He walked with his children before he returned to his kingdom. He told them this miracle would be a promise to them and future generations that he would come to rescue them when the time was right. Then they never would be separated again. They could be with him forever in the peaceful kingdom. This increased the desire deep within their soul and they were able to withstand the difficult life the villain imposed upon them. Hope was born again inside them. They encouraged each other and told many about the promise of the king. He had told them what it was like in his kingdom and they began to live that way even in their captivity. This was how their hope continued.

The king returned to his kingdom to wait for the time his children would join him. But he sent pieces of himself into the hearts of all his children to keep their hopes alive. He told the children it would guide them in truth. When the villain tried to lie to them, they would know. This would protect the truth inside and the hope that they would return to their kingdom. They would continue to live in the villain's world knowing one day it would be destroyed and they would return to living in the king's kingdom. The king would love them forever and they would live happily ever after.

This is the story of God's love for His children. It illustrates how God's enemy, Satan, lies and deceives to keep God's children away from Him. We are God's children. Satan tries to keep us away from God by offering substitutes for God's best. But God will ultimately rescue His people and take them to His kingdom forever. This is the overarching story throughout the Bible.

Our challenge is:

- To accept that God loves.
- To believe He forgives when we take the substitutes we are offered, even when we know better.
- To believe we will live forever with God in heaven.

*What did you learn from the story that you didn't know before?*


*Genesis 1: 26–31 Happy in God's kingdom*


*Genesis 2: 15–17 God provided everything, even a test of faith*

Day 4

# Whose World Is It?

## King or Villain

In yesterday's story, the children had forgotten the life they had lived in the king's world. They belonged to the king but the villain had made them slaves. The only life they knew was in the villain's world. Like us, the drama and envy enslave us but seem natural. Living that way is exhausting. Inside, we all have hope of a more peaceful life.

I believe God gives every person that hope. When the things in our world enslave us, we cry out. That's when God sends help and shows us a way out of the villain's world. But we have to act upon it.

Let's suppose yesterday's story is a Hollywood hit. Now that we know the story, let's put ourselves into the story.

## Guidelines for the Story of Your Life

Every Hollywood story has a plot, a heroine (hero) with a mission and a villain trying to interfere. In every Hollywood story, there is a struggle. The same is true with our lives. Struggle exists and the challenge is to overcome the struggle and press onward, or to give in to the struggle, allowing dreams to crash on the rocks. Triumph or tragedy.

Life is a series of struggles or you might say a miniseries of recurring elements. With each struggle, we get closer to our dreams or farther from them. When we get closer, we feel more confident. When we get farther from them, we feel disappointed. Sometimes, circumstances beyond our control spoil our dreams causing hurt and pain.

Whatever your story, as a Christian, it will include the plot of God, as the King, restoring a lost relationship with you, the heroine, and Satan as the detrimental force of the villain. You will experience either victory or defeat in every struggle. But you get a lifetime to keep trying for victory. God does not want any of our lives to end in defeat. As a Christian, God will help you in the struggles, giving confidence that you are not alone.

## The Mission

The mission is to have a restored relationship with God. Desiring to go our own way rather than go God's way separates us from God and causes a broken relationship with Him. The Bible refers to this as sin.

Not many like to be followers but most everyone likes to be a leader. It takes a lot to be a leader. It takes understanding the mission, clear communication about the mission, then encouragement and guidance to accomplish the mission. God gave us all three of those. He gave us the Bible, our guidebook, so we can understand the mission. He gave us Jesus as an example who clearly communicated the mission in person. And He gave us the Holy Spirit to guide and encourage us to accomplish the mission.

What if you were the leader of humankind? What would be your mission? Think about how difficult it would be to formulate the mission, clearly communicate that mission, and give guidance and encouragement for humankind to accomplish the mission. It would be impossible. That's why we need God to be the leader.

It's easy to follow God as the leader. He never changes. His ways have been the same since the beginning. His values are always the same. The things that change are cultures and societies. They have tried to interpret God to suit them. This has brought a lot of confusion as man has attempted to interpret the mission of God and the plan for our lives. And as humankind, we find it easier to follow man rather than God because we can see man but we can't see God. But God desires that we follow Him. He wants us to have a restored relationship with Him, and He will show us how to do it. That path is as individual as we are. That is why no man is capable of what only God can do.

## The Script

Most real life heroines don't follow a script like movie heroines. In real life, it's more like improvisation. We make it up as we go. We make somewhere around 35,000 decisions per day. We have choice. It's called free will. God made us that way. He didn't want us to be robots or clones. He wanted uniquely created individuals creating scripts for our lives that would bring Him pleasure. He wants to laugh, smile, and be pleased with what He has created.

Think of the Bible as our guidebook for creating our own scripts for life. The Protestant Bible contains sixty-six books by 40 authors. It is considered the best-selling book of all time, continuing to sell about 100 million copies per year. It has been a major influence on literature and history, especially in the Western civilization where it was first printed. If it weren't so important, it wouldn't still be around, influencing our lives.

Sure, it's full of history and other people's stories. We should use their stories as examples. But ultimately, we all write our own script. We all star in the role of life. The Bible is the guidebook for doing life. Living according to its direction gives the ability to have a life of reward and to overcome tragedy with triumph.

## What Guides You, Religion or Relationship?

Religions are meant to give meaning to life or to explain the origin of life or the universe. They tend to derive morality, ethics, religious laws or a preferred lifestyle from their ideas about the cosmos and human nature. The list of religions is exhaustive, so determining which one to live by is just as exhaustive. Many give up trying to know what to believe. But unless you know what you believe, you won't have a solid foundation on which to build your life.

> *Religion is man's attempt to explain God. If we could explain God then we would be God.*

The message and the mission of Jesus was that we could have a relationship rather than a religion. Jesus came to tell the Jews that they needed something better than the laws of Moses. The laws had served their purpose by establishing their religious culture. Jesus said he came to tell us we could have a relationship with God. In doing so, we could have a meaningful life, not just guided by rules and regulations but guided by the love of God in our hearts. Jesus told the people if they would believe in God and set their hearts to follow Him in all of His ways, He would guide them by His Holy Spirit that He would place inside of them. In that way, we could love Him, accept ourselves, and love others like He loves us. In other words, we could stop trying to be good enough for God and stop being critical of ourselves and others. When we follow God with all our hearts, it will inspire others. We won't need to convince them our way is the right way.

Is it really that simple? I believe it is. It has to be simple in order that anyone from any period in history, from any culture, or from any walk of life could know God. He loves all His children and He doesn't want anyone to meet death without knowing Him.

Spend some time thinking about what you believe. If you accept someone else's beliefs without thinking, then you will not be able to back it up. It will only be with your mouth and not your heart. It's okay if you have questions. This is where prayer comes in. Ask God to help you. In a relationship, He will give you guidance.

*I Believe...*

At the end of the 33 days, revisit your beliefs. Consider any changes you have discovered during the process.

*I Believe...*

*Date:* _____   *Signed:* _____

*Day 5*

# A Friend in High Places
## God Wants to Be Our Friend

The Latin and Greek origin of the word friend means, one you love. The German origin means peace. According to those origins, a friend is someone you love and are in a peaceful relationship with. Unfortunately, today's world reduces friend to mean simply an acquaintance. How many Facebook friends do you have? But how many of those Facebook friends do you know, love, and are in a peaceful relationship with?

It is said, "In order to have a friend, you have to be a friend." Friendships don't continue without an effort put forth to know each other. How can you know someone unless you spend time with them? Spending time reading about them on Facebook—what they like, what they do, who they hang with—is not spending time with them. Reading what someone has written means you get the manufactured version where there is time to construct an image. On Facebook, people can present themselves any way they want. But spending time with someone face to face gives you a better sense of who they are and them of who you are.

The same is true about God and reading the Bible. Reading about the things He has done in the lives of others is not the same as spending time with Him. You can know about Him and His character by reading but when you spend time with God, you will make Him your friend. Did you know God's plan is to lead us into a peaceful and loving relationship with Him? In the beginning, humankind existed in a peaceful relationship with God. God created earth and He created humankind to live in and rule over it. What a gift! In the beginning, humankind didn't question God's love. But God desires our love in return. He created humankind with a will whereby we could deliberately choose to love Him.

## God Friends Humankind in the Tabernacle

The universe is vast, infinite; without beginning or end. We refer to it as the heavens. We believe somewhere out there is God. It is impossible to understand. But God wanted to be in a relationship with humankind and he wanted to relate to us. One of the first things he did for His people was to direct them to build a place where He could meet with them. He called it the tabernacle, and it was a movable tent so they could erect it wherever they went. God gave Moses the Ten Commandments and a lot of other laws in order to establish their culture but God also wanted to live with His people.

(Read the books of Exodus, Leviticus, and Deuteronomy for the laws that helped develop the nation for the people God called His.)

God asked the people, through Moses, to bring an offering of "gold, silver and brass, and blue and purple, and scarlet, and fine linen and goats' hair, and rams' skins dyed red and badgers' skins and acacia wood, and oil for the light, and spices for anointing oil, and the sweet incense, and onyx stones" (Exodus 35:5b–9a, KJV).

(Read Exodus 35–40 if you want to how God directed them to make this tabernacle.)

The point is, God wanted a place to meet with His people, and He wanted them to contribute to it. Relationships are a two-way street. When the people finished the tabernacle, God inhabited it. The book of Exodus says it like this: "Then a cloud covered the tent of the congregation, and the glory of the Lord filled the tabernacle" (Exodus 40:34, KJV). The cloud was a sign of God's presence.

## God Friends Humankind in the Temple

God's people were nomads in the early days. Forty years after being slaves in Egypt, God led them into a land of their own. They had several kings before one decided the tabernacle should be a permanent place. It was called Solomon's temple, named after its builder. He built this temple according to the same layout God had given Moses, but it was much more elaborate. It included all the same elements that gave access to God. Access to God in those days came through animal sacrifices and offerings, and through an in-between person—the priest. God had given His people specific instructions in order to meet with Him. God's presence came in a cloud when the temple was finished, the same way it had come the first time. "Then the house was filled with a cloud…for the glory of the Lord had filled the house of God" (2 Chronicles 5:13b, 14a, KJV).

## God Friends Humankind in Our Heart

After Jesus came, we had a different way to have access to God. It became possible to be in a personal relationship with God. 1 John: 1 – 4 is an eyewitness account of the way in which this became possible. In both tabernacles, the tent and the temple, God came as a cloud. But in Jesus, God came as a man. He made Himself human in order for us to see Him and understand Him on human terms. The cloud made Him untouchable. But as a human, we could become His friend. The tabernacle, or the place to meet with God, went from being a tent, to a temple, to the heart of a person.

So it stands to reason that if we want to be friends with God, we should accept the way in which He made that possible. The person of Jesus must become our friend. It's easier to understand being in a relationship with a person than being in relationship with a cloud.

## God Wants to Be Your Friend

Oh, you say, Jesus is not living today so how can we be His friend? This is what makes it possible. When Jesus departed earth, He left His friends with a promise. "I am going to send you what my Father has promised; but stay in the city until you have been clothed with power from on high" (Luke 24:49, NIV).

So what was that promise? Jesus appeared to His friends after His death and said, "Do not leave Jerusalem, but wait for the gift my Father promised, which you have heard me speak about. For John baptized with water, but in a few days you will be baptized with the Holy Spirit" (Acts 1:4b–5, NIV). "All of them were filled with the Holy Spirit" (Acts 2:4, NIV).

In other words, to those people who waited for the promise, God gave a piece of Himself. It was in the form of His spirit to live inside them. But it is for God's purpose that He does this. "But you will receive power when the Holy Spirit comes on you; and you will be my witnesses in Jerusalem, and in Judea and Samaria, and to the ends of the earth" (Acts 1:8, NIV).

## Why God Wants to Be Your Friend

What is God's purpose? It is to restore the lost inheritance of humankind's relationship with Him. In this way, God's kingdom will come to earth. One by one, in the hearts of individuals, who trust Him enough to follow His ways, His kingdom will come.

What steps should we take in developing this relationship? First, simply believe God wants to be in a relationship with us. Then there must be an appointed meeting place and time. We do that with other friends, why not with God? This is different than going to church or Bible studies. Those activities are where we learn about God's ways. It's like going to a party. When there are others in the room, the dynamics are different. We need to spend time one on one with someone in order to know them.

## Making Friends with God

I suggest making a meeting place. It could be anywhere but be intentional about it. I have a favorite overstuffed khaki tweed chair in my office. On it is my favorite red pillow to support my back and a giraffe print throw for my shoulders if it is chilly. When I want to meet with God, I go there. Sometimes I like to change it up and go to a park for a walk with Him. But I don't like any interference from my phone or other noise. And I know from experience God doesn't like to compete for our attention. God is the still, small voice inside. We have to be listening to actually hear Him.

Your next challenge is to make a time when you will meet with God. Choose a time when it will be quiet. Go to your meeting place each day for a time with God. Allow Him to talk to you through the pages of the Bible and through His Spirit and let Him know what you are feeling or thinking in prayer. Last but not least, write it down. It's easy to forget how God encourages us, but in writing it down, we can go back and remember His faithfulness. In this way, your belief and trust will grow. You will become friends with God.

*Your mission today:*

- *Decide on a meeting place*
- *Decide on a time of day to meet with God*
- *Get a Bible and a journal for your time with God*

Day 6

# Citizens of Two Worlds

## Being in Two Places at the Same Time

The Bible talks about two worlds. The world we see with our eyes and the unseen world. I refer to the world we see with our eyes as Hollywood. I refer to the unseen world as heaven. Our physical bodies exist in the world influenced by Hollywood and our spirit exists in the world influenced by heaven. Our soul exists in the in-between. So, we are made up of three parts—body, spirit, and soul.

## Are We Two or Three–People?

Most religious or spiritual teachings suggest humans are two-dimensional beings, comprised of body and soul. The body is the material part of humans and the soul is the immaterial part. The body is how we navigate earth and how others perceive us. The soul is the immaterial part of humans comprised of thought, emotion, and behavior.

## Becoming Three-Dimensional

As Christians, we view ourselves as three-dimensional creatures—body, soul, and spirit. The third dimension comes into existence when we accept what the Bible says by believing in God's kingdom. That is when we begin to be motivated by something other than *our* own soul, what *we* think, what *we* want, or how something makes *us* feel.

    We begin to identify with God and what He wants for us as individuals and as humankind, not simply our own desires. This third part is born into existence and occupied by an internal moral compass, God's spirit inside us. It directs us to identify with God and what He wants for us as individuals and as humankind. That is why our salvation experience is called "born again". We are born once as body and soul, and a second time when the spirit of God comes alive in us to give guidance in this life.

As Christians, I propose we look at ourselves as three-dimensional creatures—body, soul, and spirit. The third dimension is experienced when you accept or believe in God, accept His forgiveness for living a life separated from Him, and begin to be motivated by something other than your own soul, what you think, what you want, or how something makes you feel.

## The Trinity: Three-Dimensional

The first book of the Bible, Genesis, tells us that God created humans in His likeness. He is referred to as the Trinity and expressed as God, Jesus, and the Holy Spirit. *God* was the spirit that gave Jesus a sense of purpose or reason for living. *Jesus* was the physical body God inhabited when He lived with humankind. The *Holy Spirit* was the soul who gave Jesus a unique expression of God while He walked on earth. So it stands to reason "in His likeness" means we also have a spirit, body, and soul.

Without God's spirit, we are two-dimensional beings. Without His spirit alive in us, we will put our self at center when it comes to desires. We make decisions in terms of the satisfaction, or pain it brings us. We go after what we want and feel is our right, according to each individual's standards. With self-centered desires, we are subject to behavior like judgment of others, being the victim, manipulating others or allowing oneself to be manipulated, arguing to convince others of ones desires, and greed, just to name a few. Simply put, it means the only guide we have is our own feelings, thoughts, and emotions.

## The Third Dimension, Love

When we invite God to live inside us, we add the third dimension of the spirit. This takes us out of center and puts God's spirit at the center. It means we process the world in terms of how it satisfies God, not ourselves. That does not mean we are robots without desires. It means that our soul, which is our unique expression on earth, is subject to God. When we put God at the center, it means we allow His influences on our character which drives our behavior. We take on His character traits using the unique personalities and physical structures we possess. Then we become an extension of Him in the earth. We have the ability to live outside of our selfish desires and consider others.

When we live outside of our selfish desires and consider others, it is called love. In the Bible, we are told that we are not capable of loving others without God to influence us.

> My beloved friends let us continue to love each other since love comes from God. Everyone who loves is born of God and experiences a relationship with God. The person who refuses to love doesn't know the first thing about God, because God is love—so you can't know him if you don't love.
>
> —1 John 4:7–8, MSG

## Heaven Kind of Love

Heaven's culture puts God as the center of attention and yourself second. Heaven kind of love means you are thinking of others; you've got their back and they have yours. You stand up for them, think the best of them, support them in their efforts, give them the biggest piece, think more of them than yourself, let them go first, don't want what they have but are proud of them for what they have, don't keep score of whose better, don't smirk when they are wrong, don't force your thinking on them, don't get angry but look for truth in every situation and always think the best of them. That's the God kind of love. What if everyone loved like that? It would be a different world. This is what the Bible says about developing a godly character.

> *Love never gives up, cares more for others than for self, doesn't want what it doesn't have, doesn't strut, doesn't have a swelled head, doesn't force itself on others, isn't always "me first", doesn't fly off the handle, doesn't keep score of the sins of others, doesn't revel when others grovel, takes pleasure in the flowering of truth, puts up with anything, trusts God always, always looks for the best, never looks back, but keeps going to the end.*
>
> I Corinthians 13 MSG

> If everyone would love like that, it would change the world. If only some would love like that, it would still change the world. What if only one would love like that? Jesus did and it revolutionized the world. Jesus started the revolution and God's hope is that it continues in us.

## Hollywood Kind of Love

Hollywood is famous for its love stories. In some capacity, love is included in every movie and TV program. According to what the Bible says, one cannot truly love without God. So the love that Hollywood presents is the kind of love that puts self at center. Since we thrive on entertainment, we allow its message to influence us subtly.

> *In Hollywood's culture, when you love someone it means they are giving you what you need or want. As long as you are getting what you want in that relationship you remain in it. It could be a romantic, family, friendship, or business relationship, but the starring role is usually based on the needs of that person being met by something or someone else.*
>
> *It boils down to the pursuit of your own happiness.*

Many who have chased the illusions of Hollywood have been disappointed. Marilyn Monroe became an icon for Hollywood. Her sexy sizzle gave Hollywood a fresh new image and she made them millions of dollars. In the early stage of her career, her photo was on the cover of Life magazine with a quote beside it. "Do I look happy? I should—for I was a child nobody wanted. I was a lonely child with a dream—who awakened to find that dream come true. I am Marilyn Monroe. Read my Cinderella story" (Wikipedia). This young lady, raised in foster care, was desperately looking for someone who would love her and meet her needs. She was discovered by Hollywood and it gave her what she needed—an identity and a sense that she was valued. She, in return gave them what they needed, box office sales. But Hollywood's demands proved more than she could handle. Later in her career, she was quoted as saying this:

> *Hollywood is a place where they'll pay you a thousand dollars for a kiss and fifty cents for your soul.*
>
> —Marilyn Monroe

I believe from this quote she learned the identity and value Hollywood gave her was not what she needed in the long run. It gave her what she needed temporarily, but it did not give her love that would stick with her. I believe she craved a love that no one was able to give her; a love that is not self-motivating, self-satisfying, and self-centered. Eventually, she gave up trying to find that kind of love.

## Seek True Love

Humans, apart from God, are not capable of giving or receiving true love without ulterior motivation. It is human nature to seek pleasure or avoid pain. The only way possible to give and receive true love is to live a God-centered life. Jesus's message when He lived on earth was about developing a godly character motivated by love. That happens on the inside of us and we must transform our thinking process in order to do so.

*Dear God,*

*I didn't realized I have been motived by self-centeredness. I thought that's the way I was supposed to make decisions. By what I wanted, needed, or desired. I didn't realize that you wanted to be the center of my world.*

*Now that I know, please help me to know what you want. I want to please you in my actions. Because you love me, you already know my needs. I want to leave those secret desires for you to help me with.*

*Help me put you at the center of my thinking. I want to consider you and what pleases you first. Then I believe you will help me with my life. Help me trust you to bring the best for me.*

_____
_____
_____
_____
_____
_____

*Day 7*

# A New Heart for a New Start

## Our Hearts

We have two hearts. One is a blood pump and the other is our brain. But science says that our heart is more than a pump, it also triggers emotion. The heart has its own nervous system and the chemicals produced in the brain affect the heart. Our heart and our brain are connected. The heart and the brain are in constant communication.

How we feel affects how we think and how we think affects how we feel. When we feel an emotion, we begin to process it in our brain. We go back and forth, the heart checking with the brain and the brain checking with the heart. Our heart guides our thoughts, but our thoughts directly affect our heart. In turn, our bodies are affected. Toxic thoughts can weaken our immune system. That's why we will likely be sick when we deal with emotional stress.

Science confirms the connection between your emotions and your thoughts. The more we are able to manage our thoughts, the more we will be able to deal constructively with our emotions.

If we deal with disappointments with emotions only, it can change our thinking. But if we change our thinking, it will help balance our emotions. Changing our thinking is the way to change our reality. But how do we do that? By learning to see things the way God has intended.

## Dealing with False Hopes

Can you recall a time in your life when you felt safe? Everything was peaceful, there was no stress, and you could laugh out loud with joy in your heart? Depending on the circumstances you were born into, you may remember this as childhood. But at some point, we realize that life is not fair. That is usually at a time when we begin to observe others and compare our lives to theirs.

Initially, we compare ourselves to others physically—what we look like, what we wear, where we live, and how our family compares to other families. But eventually, we will compare our relationships to the relationships that others have. In other words, what does love look like between a man and a woman? What do friendships look like? What do job relationships look like between a boss and employer or between coworkers?

Hollywood gives us plenty to compare with. We watch movies and shows, observe celebrities, and read the tweets about their lives and relationships. We pattern our responses after their responses. If we like a particular movie or celebrity, we will likely respond in the same way they have when in similar circumstances.

As much as we hope relationships and circumstances will be perfect, we find they are not. Then we experience disappointment. Below are four ways we might deal with disappointment based on the book *Enemies of the Heart* by Andy Stanley.

## Dealing with Disappointment

- *Jealousy*. Says "God owes me." We compare what we have with what others have and feel life isn't fair. You may feel like they are better looking, have nicer things, better jobs, or more friends. You may not blame them but somehow you feel that God skipped you when he gave out the best. You think God owes you something more than what you have.

- *Anger*. Says "you owe me." Your circumstances haven't been fair and you feel like someone owes you because of it. You feel your circumstances aren't your fault, it's someone else's fault. You hold onto hurts caused from people in the past even if they aren't still in your life. You are angry for being cheated in life and feel like someone owes you because of it.

- *Guilt*. Says "I owe you." Somehow, you feel like you have done something wrong. You feel like you have a debt or a burden that you must satisfy. You feel that if you do good things for others, give to charities, or serve in church you can work it off. You don't feel forgiven and you must do something about it.

- *Greed*. Says "I owe me." You are afraid you won't get what you want. If you don't work hard then you're not going to get it. You work hard for what you have and will continue to do so to get what you want. You don't trust God, you feel you must do it yourself. You hold onto what you have. You feel you deserve the best and you're going to get it.

## Help With Disappointments

Without the reality of God, we will deal with disappointments mostly with emotions. But when we include God and begin to see things from a different perspective, we can learn to deal with disappointment differently.

God created us. He knows all the circumstances of our lives. He knows our thoughts and our feelings. He created us with two brains. Science is just making the connection between our hearts and our thoughts but God has always known.

> You watched me as I was being formed in utter seclusion, as I was woven together in the dark of the womb. You saw me before I was born. Every day of my life was recorded in your book. Every moment was laid out before a single day had passed. How precious are your thoughts about me, Oh, God.
>
> —Psalm 139: 15–17a NLT

Because God knows us and loves us, He wants us to be whole. God can heal our disappointment, but we have to allow Him to change the way we think. It will be different than the way Hollywood thinks.

Keep in mind we are each unique individuals. There are no two people who are exactly alike. Identical twins even have differences. God reminds us of our individuality by our unique set of fingerprints. There are no two that are exactly alike. Because of that, it is important to realize we all react differently to disappointment. We may talk it over with friends but when it comes right down to it, we need to talk it over with God.

But generally speaking, if we take our eyes off our hurts and ask God to heal our hearts, he will start with our thoughts. Remember, right thinking can affect our heart positively and we can reverse the negative emotions from our hearts that have caused wrong thinking. By learning to think according to what the Bible says about God's love for us, we can move past our disappointments. If we don't move past them, they will come up throughout our lives and it may establish a pattern. It will keep us from forgiving others and ourselves.

> If you forgive other people when they sin against you,
> your heavenly Father will also forgive you.
> But if you do not forgive others their sins, your Father will not forgive your sins.
> —Matthew 6: 14–15 NIV

## Ask for Help

When God heals our shattered hearts, we can come to Him with a whole heart. Allow the Bible to transform your thinking. Learn to think heaven's way when it comes to disappointments.

When something happens to disappoint you, ask God for a new way to view it. Ask Him how to change your thinking so it isn't destructive. Jealousy, guilt, anger, and greed are not God's ways. They lead to strife, not peace. Seek peace as you talk to God about your disappointments. He will show you things like this that are counterculture:

- Jealousy. The way to deal with jealousy is to be happy for others.
- Anger. The way to deal with anger is to forgive others.
- Guilt. The way to deal with guilt is to accept God's forgiveness.
- Greed. The way to deal with greed is trust God's provision.

> So get rid of all evil behavior. Be done with all deceit, hypocrisy, jealousy, and all unkind speech.
>
> —1 Peter 2:1

*Dear God,*

*I have found myself dealing with disappointment with _____. (from the four listed above) I want to trust you with my heart. I want to change my thinking so my emotions don't always get their way. Help me learn to deal with my disappointments so they are not destructive. I want to have a whole heart.*

*(Write your own prayer. Be specific about things that have disappointed you. Ask God's forgiveness.)*

Date: _____

> "Don't copy the behavior and customs of this world, but let God transform you into a new person by changing the way you think. Then you will learn to know God's will for you, which is good, and pleasing, and perfect."
>
> —Romans 12:2 NLT

Day 8

# Enter Your New Reality

## Choose Your Destination

Every successful venture begins with the end in mind. Before you know how to get someplace, you must know where you are going. Otherwise, you will wander aimlessly.

If we are to be heaven bound in a Hollywood world, we must begin with heaven as our destination. And we must begin to live like we're going there.

If you take a road trip, you begin with your destination in mind. A map or navigation system will give instructions on how to get there. If you take a wrong turn or ignore your navigation system, you won't reach your destination. If you are determined to reach your destination, you will turn around and get back on track. The same is true when heaven is our destination. We must be determined it is our destination or we will wander aimlessly.

> "Not everyone who calls out to me, 'Lord! Lord!'
> will enter the Kingdom of Heaven.
> Only those who actually do the will of my Father in heaven will enter."
>
> —Matthew 7:21 NLT

## Become a Citizen of Heaven Now

A citizen is a person who belongs to and owes loyalty to a state or nation. As citizens, we accept, uphold, and learn to live according to the laws and principals of that nation. We have the responsibility to be a contributing member when we receive the benefits of citizenship.

In America, some of the benefits of citizenship are free education, public spaces like roads and parks, representation in government, protection by military and police. But we have the responsibility to accept, uphold, and learn the laws. If we don't, we will pay whatever consequences are attached to breaking those laws. Citizens of the USA contribute toward benefits in another way—by paying taxes. Becoming a citizen is a two-way street. When we accept citizenship, we receive benefits but we also have a responsibility.

The same is true in God's kingdom of heaven. When we believe in God, accept His love and protection, then receive forgiveness for going our own way, we become citizens in God's kingdom. At that point, we become citizens of heaven. We possess dual citizenship. We are citizens of the world, but we are also citizens of the kingdom of heaven. When that happens, we have responsibilities to God's kingdom as well as to the world.

Sometimes the laws of those two worlds are in conflict. But when you are citizens of both, the overriding laws are God's laws. When you obey God's laws, you will be a good citizen of the world, but when you obey the laws of the world, you will not necessarily be a good citizen of heaven. The two are in conflict because God rules the kingdom of heaven and humankind rules the world.

Changing your reality means accepting that two worlds exist simultaneously. One is the kingdom of the world and the other is the kingdom of heaven. Humankind rules one kingdom and God rules the other kingdom.

## Learn to Live Heaven's Way

Every kingdom has its laws. That is how we are able to exist together as a society. If every person did what he or she wanted to do, it would be difficult to exist together. There would be no pattern of behavior, making it difficult to trust others or to know what's expected. For example, what if everyone did what they wanted to do at a traffic light? If red didn't mean stop and green didn't mean go, there would be chaos.

God's kingdom has laws. They started as the Ten Commandments. We are very familiar with them. But God gave Moses (who penned the Ten Commandments on tablets of stone) many other laws, too. God gave them to Moses in order to establish His nation—a society based on love with God as the ruler king.

By the time Jesus came to live on earth, these laws had been interpreted and reinterpreted so many times that it became difficult to follow them. Even the spiritual leaders of the day argued about the laws. You would have thought that ten simple laws would have been easy to follow.

> The Ten Commandments
>
> 1. Have no God but me
> 2. Don't worship idols
> 3. Don't misuse God's name
> 4. Observe the Sabbath and keep it holy
> 5. Honor your father and your mother
> 6. Don't murder
> 7. Don't commit adultery
> 8. Don't steal
> 9. Don't tell lies about others
> 10. Don't lust after what others have

Jesus told the religious leaders of the day they had made the laws too difficult to follow. It made people depend on learning the laws and not on living the laws. They were frustrated because there were too many laws and it became difficult to live by them. That sounds a little like today, doesn't it?

But Jesus wanted to make things simple for us. He wanted to make it easy to understand God's ways. He spoke before a crowd and He summed up heaven's standards like this.

> "Here's a simple, rule-of-thumb guide for behavior: Ask yourself what you want people to do for you, then grab the initiative and do it for them.
>
> Add up God's law [God's written commandments] and the Prophets [God's spoken commandments] and this is what you get."
>
> —Matthew 7: 12 MSG
>
> *(We know this as "The Golden Rule" – Do to others what you would have them do to you.)*

## Put Forth the Effort

If you don't put any effort into learning how to change the way you think, it will be difficult to live according to heaven's standards. You will live by the world's standards because you will learn from those around you and not from God. But Jesus sent a helper when he left earth. He is the Holy Spirit. He is God's spirit, alive in us, to guide us toward His truth. He is there whenever we invite God to live in us. We can call on Him for help.

Learning to know God's will for your life requires effort on your part. I've discovered a simple method that will increase the more you practice it. Benedictine monks practiced it centuries ago, but it continues to be a very effective method for making the Bible personal and not just a bunch of do's and don'ts. It will also help grow a relationship with God as you allow Him to speak to you through the Bible.

First, go to your special place with your Bible and your journal. Clear your mind of all distractions. Focus on God. This takes practice. We are accustomed to letting our mind wander in all directions. Say a simple prayer inviting God into your thoughts and asking the Holy Spirit to reveal God's thoughts.

When you feel like you are ready, choose a couple of verses from the Bible. If you are new at this, I suggest choosing verses from Psalms or Proverbs. They aren't from a story or history lesson so you won't necessarily need to know the context of the verses. Select two to four verses to read to begin with. Reading too many verses will cause you to lose your focus.

> *Four Steps to Discover what the Bible says Personally*
>
> - *Read*
>   Slowly read the verses, focusing on the words as you read them. Read them again slowly. Read them a third time. A few words or passage should begin to stand out. Read the verses a fourth time, paying particular attention to the words that stand out. Record the verses and words in your journal.
>
> - *Meditate*
>   Take the words that stand out into your mind. Think about what they mean. Allow your thoughts to wander where they will. Your mind is making connections with the verses. Write your thoughts in your journal.
>
> - *Pray*
>   Speak to God. Have a conversation (like you would with a friend) about the verses you've read and what you felt as you meditated on them. Give God thanks as you ask Him to show you how they apply to your life. You may want to write your prayer in your journal.
>
> - *Contemplate*
>   This is a time of silence when you ponder the verses and the personal meaning they have to you. Think about how they will make a difference in your life. Journal your thoughts.

*My Discovery of what the Bible says to me:*
*Read: (Your Verses)*
_____
_____
_____


*Meditate: (Which word or phrase stands out?)*
_____
_____


*Pray: (Invite God to show you what this means for your life.)*
_____
_____
_____


*Contemplate: (How will these verses affect your thinking or behavior?)*
_____
_____
_____
_____
_____
_____

## Ask for God's Help

You can know the entire Bible, memorize it, quote it, use it as a weapon against others, but if you don't allow God's Holy Spirit to show you how to apply it to your life and change your life, then the Bible is just words on a page.

But these words can come alive, they can energize and they can transform your life when you ask God to interpret them to you personally and then put them into action.

> For the word of God is alive and active. Sharper than any double-edged sword,
> it penetrates even to dividing soul and spirit, joints and marrow;
> it judges the thoughts and attitudes of the heart.
>
> —Heb. 4:12 NIV

## Change Your Reality

Changing your reality means you must become aware of another way other than your present reality. Believe in the reality of the kingdom of heaven, make it your destination, then live like you're going there.

The message of the world is very strong and loud. It is the message of self-satisfaction. It is self-reliant, beginning and ending with you and what you are able to do.

The message of heaven is found in silence, in a whisper. The message of heaven is God satisfaction. It is God-reliant, beginning and never-ending with God and what He is able to do in and through our lives.

To change one's reality, one must have a mind-set to pursue living heaven's ways in a Hollywood world.

*Dear God,*

*Help me pursue your ways. I want to hear you. I want to learn your ways. I want to have purpose and aim in my life. Help me:*

_____
_____
_____
_____
_____
_____
_____
_____
_____
_____
_____
_____
_____
_____

*Date:* _____

# CHALLENGE 2

## Change Your Identity

# A New You

Is it possible to see things with new eyes? Yes it is. When we accept new information, we are likely to change our minds from the way we previously viewed something.

For example, the illustration below confirms this idea.

Looking at the picture, do you see an old woman or a young woman?
Your answer: _____

Most everyone sees a hat or scarf with a feather and some dark hair. Where we differ in is in the center of the drawing. You will either see an eye or an ear below the dark hair.

If you see an ear then below it you will see a line indicating the jaw of a young woman. Below the feather and the hair, you will see eyelashes and a nose. She appears to be wearing a necklace and a fur collar.

If you see an eye, then below it you will see a line indicating a nose. Below the nose, you will see a line indicating a mouth. She also appears to be wearing a fur collar.

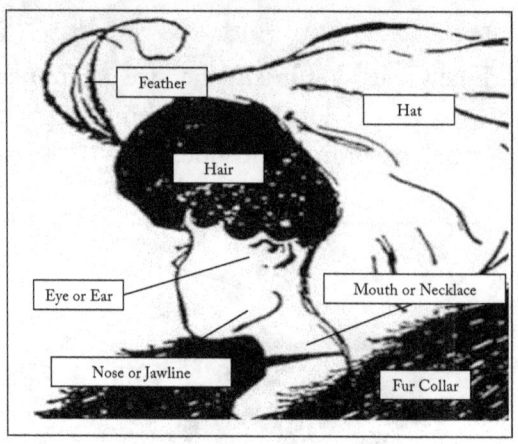

## One and One Equals Three

Now that you have been introduced to new information you can see how it is possible to view things differently than you did. On day six, we discovered that when we accept God into our lives, we become three-dimensional. That is new math—one and one equals three.

*1 - ME (Body & Soul)*
*+ 1 - GOD (Spirit)*
―――――――――――――
*3 Dimensions of Humanity*

We are born as body and soul; with an outside and an inside. We are bones, muscle, organs, blood, and skin. But what gives our body action comes from inside; it is mind, will, and emotion. Most people agree that there are two dimensions to human beings: appearance and behavior. I call this our Skinside and our Inside.

We include a third dimension, our Deeperside, when we accept God into our lives. It is the spiritual dimension born into existence the moment we realize we are going our own way and separated from God. When we regret not including God, accept God's love and forgiveness, and begin to include Him in the decisions of our lives, we begin to live a different way. We invite God to come live in us. We ask for Him to motivate our behavior rather than be motivated by our own soul.

The Bible gives evidence of this third dimension. Jesus explained this difficult concept to a prominent Jewish leader named Nicodemus. He knew Jesus's insightful teachings and miracles pointed to something greater than humanity and it was God. Jesus told him it was only possible to understand the things of God's kingdom if you were born a second time, of the spirit. He explained we are born once from our mother's womb but the second birth of the spirit means to come out of living in the darkness, hiding our immoral attitudes and ways, and begin living in the light of God's truth.

Accepting this way of life gives guidance and creates security. It means you're not making it up as you go. You accept God's way of doing things and try to apply them to your life. You can read the entire story of Nicodemus for yourself in John 3:1–21.

In living a two-dimensional life, self is at the center. There is no other guide except one's own soul. Therefore, the mind, will, and emotions of the individual will rule their behavior. Without the spirit alive is us, we live our lives in terms of how it satisfies our own desires. We will go after what we want and feel is our right. You've heard the phrases, "I'm looking out for number one", "If it feels good, do it", "It's all about me". They mean the same thing; that you approach life getting your needs met and creating standards whereby you will achieve what you want. You might break laws or timeless moral codes in order to justify self-satisfaction. This is what Jesus meant by living in darkness. He said when we add the third dimension of the spirit, we come into the light, not ashamed, so our deeds can be seen by all.

Adding the third dimension of the spirit takes soul out of center and puts God at the center. We will begin to process our lives and our circumstances in terms of how it satisfies God, not ourselves.

We allow godly values to influence our character and that's what motivates our behavior. We take on godly character traits while using the unique personalities and physical structures we possess. Then we become an extension of Him in the earth. We have the ability to live outside of our selfish desires.

But it also implies trust in a God we can't see. The more we develop a personal relationship with Him, the more we will trust Him. We tend to be shortsighted. We can only see what's happening right now, or know what's happened in the past. We can't tell the future. We will likely make decisions based on knowing the past and the present. Not the future. And our future is the most important part. It is the part where we need God's help. If we can truly believe what the Bible says, we can learn to trust God.

> For I know the plans I have for you says the Lord, they are plans for good and not for disaster, to give you a future and a hope.
>
> —Jerimiah 29: 11 NIV

Learning to change our identity means learning to view our Skinside, Inside, and Deeperside according to God's view, not our own view. In order to do so, we need to know what God says. In other words, gaining new information (what God says) will help us view things differently. It will help us view our Skinside, Inside, and Deeperside according to God. It is contrary to what current culture says. But once we get God's view of us, we will be able to understand our purposes in life. Then we will be able to develop our *Otherside*, where we become partners with God in order to share His love with others.

> *We are not all capable of the same thing*
> *But, we are all capable of some thing.*

Day 10

## **Skinside: Your Body**

"Oh my gosh! I can't believe it. The president of the United States is coming to stay at my house!"

"Shut up! How is that possible?"

"Well, I entered my name in a sort of, well, online contest. I had to agree my place would be available long term for an ongoing experiment of some kind, and that I would be available for chats every day with him."

"This can't really be happening. I mean he has the White House. Why would he want to stay at your place? And what kind of experiment is it anyway?

"I don't know. I read he's trying to get in touch with the people. You know, everyday kind of people. He said he thinks he's been around politicians for so long that he's out of touch with what people really want."

"Are we talking about the real president? 'Cause this sounds bogus to me."

"I know, but the secret service guys have already been here to check things out."

"No way!"

"Yeah, way. I mean, at first I was skeptical but they came to my job and checked that out, too. They said I'd have Secret Service protection, too. You know not everybody likes the president."

"Yeah, but he's still the most powerful man in the world. You gotta respect that."

"No kidding. But anyway, he's coming next week."

"Next week? How long is he staying?"

"Not sure. But I'm supposed to continue my normal life. Oh, and get this. I've gotta cook dinner every night, too. He may or may not be there to eat it, but I gotta cook it."

"Where is he going to sleep?"

"In my bedroom. I'm gonna stay in the spare room 'cause my bed is the best one. I couldn't have him sleep on that lousy mattress."

"Is he gonna, like, take over your house? 'Cause if he is, you gotta change some of your habits. Like picking up your dirty clothes instead of leaving them all around the house."

"Yeah, I know. The secret service guys said he's going to be like a guest and I'm supposed to treat him like I would anyone else. And I'd pick up dirties for anybody else."

"Yeah, right. Like the president is just anybody else."

"I know. It really feels weird. It makes me wanna get new stuff. Like I want him to experience the best while he's here."

"Ohh, shopping. I love to shop. Can I come?"

"Sure. I could use the help. I'm thinking new bed linens, towels, and maybe a new rug in my bedroom. Gotta change that burned out lightbulb, too. I want to make sure he feels cozy. You know, it's gotta be weird for him, too. He doesn't know me."

"Yeah, but I'm sure you'll have time to get to know each other. Especially if you're going to have dinner with him every night. You've gotta talk about something."

"What if he doesn't like me?"

"Well, I'd make sure he does like you. By the way, are you getting paid for this?"

"Uh, no. I never ever thought about that. I just thought it was a privilege to have him stay here."

"Yeah, you're right. Imagine that. Getting to know the president, personally. Wow! You'll have some story to tell your grandkids."

"I guess I'm not the only one who he's going to stay with. The secret service guys said he's picked a lot of people out of the contest. They said a few people refused when they found out the details of his stay but most people were excited about it."

"Like what details?"

"Well, I kinda have to be his representative in a neighborhood group."

"Okay, now this changes things. I thought you only had to cook dinner."

"I know. But it really sounds like a good thing. He's just trying to get to know people. I guess he feels so out of touch with real people that he wants to use common folk, like me, to tell them what he's really like."

"That sounds pretty good. I mean, he can't really be as bad as the media makes him sound. But taking over your house…are you okay with that?"

"I guess you could say, I'm honored. I mean, I'm nobody. And the president of the United States is going to become, sort of, well, a friend."

"I wonder what favors you might get in the future. Imagine, you get in some trouble and you call him up. "Hey, Pres, ol' friend. Remember me? I'm the one who cooked spaghetti every night.""

"All I can say is I'm nervous and excited at the same time. I know all my time, attention, and energy is going into this."

Try to imagine the president of the United States is coming to stay at your home. What would you do? You would try to make it as nice as possible. You might clean it, get new stuff, or quit some annoying habits. You would want to impress him. You'd want him to like you in case you needed favors in the future. You would tell others what kind of person he is. Right?

Try to imagine the God of the universe coming to stay inside you. What would you do? You would want your body to be as nice as you could if you knew he would be living there for a while. You'd want him to like you. You would tell others what kind of person he is. Right?

But do we? Do we think of our bodies as something we share with God? Most of us don't. We think of our body only as our own. We think God lives out in the clouds or in the wind. We don't think about Him living inside us. But He does. His spirit, His Holy Spirit dwells within us daily. Just take a minute to think about that. The God of the universe walks about on planet earth in us, each of us who invite Him in.

> And so, dear brothers and sisters, I plead with you to give your bodies
> to God because of all he has done for you.
> Let them be a living and holy sacrifice—the kind he will find acceptable.
> This is truly the way to worship him.
>
> —Romans 12:1 NLT

Spend some time thinking about what you could do differently knowing you share your body with God? (Journal your thoughts.)

_____
_____
_____
_____

Day 11

# Skinside: Hollywood Says

Our body is our identity. It is how we present ourselves to the world. And it's a very competitive world. How are we to get noticed? How will we gain recognition? How will someone value us? Hollywood says it's through our body.

We put major emphasis on our body because it is the visual part of who we are. It's how others see us. Our body says something about us. It says what we spend our time and money on. Exercising, shopping, going to the spa or plastic surgeon, eating, or _____. It's our identity.

Why are we so obsessed with our bodies? Because we know other's opinion of us is riding on it. We care what others think of us. And Hollywood sets the standard for that. Hollywood images define what's expected of us.

## Beautiful Women

Every woman desires to be beautiful. The beauty industry is a multimillion dollar industry because we hope, with help, we can be beautiful. Fashion and beauty enhancements are fun, creative, and they do help us express who we are to others. They help us to be pleasing and desirable.

Beauty is desirable. Whether it is in art, nature, or the human body, it has always been pleasing to gaze upon. Beauty is comprised of balance and color, creating harmony and something to enjoy. God created beauty for His pleasure, so it stands to reason we would enjoy beauty, too. (Because He lives in us.)

## Discontent

Where it goes wrong is when envy comes in. When we become discontent and resentment is aroused by a desire for the possessions or qualities of someone else, then it can become destructive. There are certain physical qualities about us that are God-given. Rather than accept what those are, sometimes we resent them and wish for something else.

Longing for something better is stealing our contentment. Hollywood promotes an endless supply of beauty and better circumstances. Constantly viewing those images helps create discontentment. Have you ever said, "I wish I _____."

Simply wishing for something better doesn't have to be all bad. Wishing for better circumstances in life has caused many to become successful. But when it comes to our bodies, we can't control everything or wish away our genetic makeup. We inherit those traits. Some things we are better off accepting.

Envy is a driving force that causes some to take action. Even when it comes to genetics, we can alter them, in some cases. A most extreme case on television was a sixteen-year-old girl who didn't like being short. She wanted to be tall so badly that she had bone implants in her legs to make her four inches taller. Do you think others liked her better four inches taller or did they value her more? We can't really say for sure but what we do know for sure is that God didn't care whether she was four inches taller. He loved her short.

So why is other's opinion of us more important than God's opinion? We sometimes place more importance on what a stranger thinks of us than what God thinks of us. God is not as judgmental as humans. We measure each other by different standards than God does.

Hollywood says we have to be beautiful, skinny, and rich to gain acceptance. They publicly crucify anyone who doesn't meet that criteria. So what are we to think and feel? We believe if we don't meet that criteria, then we won't be accepted either. Our conscious mind knows that isn't true but in our subconscious we believe that we have to be perfect in order to have value.

## What Drives Our Behavior?

The search for acceptance is a very basic need in all humans. At our core, we desire to be loved and valued. When we don't have someone in our life who meets that need, we will settle for anyone to meet that need. And because subconsciously we believe the lie that perfection equals acceptance, we are likely to do anything to our bodies and with our bodies to achieve whatever we believe it takes. We are seeking to be loved and valued by someone.

The risk with desiring to be valued by others is twofold.

- We will do anything to gain acceptance; anything that is required from that other person or group of people.

- We desire to be worshiped; no, not by someone bowing down on their knees but by someone being completely and utterly devoted to us.

This is sometimes how we use our body. We don't think of it as God's house, we think we can use it in whatever way we want to gain acceptance and value from others. Other times, we don't like ourselves and we take it out on our body. We feel that no one else cares about us so why should we. We use our bodies to sin. That means we commit an offense against God or violate His ways.

> Do not let any part of your body become an instrument of evil to serve sin.
> Instead, give yourselves completely to God,
> for you were dead, but now you have new life.
> So use your whole body as an instrument to do what is right for the glory of God.
> —Romans 6:13 NLT

Are there ways you are sinning against God with your body?

_____
_____
_____
_____
_____
_____

God is faithful to forgive us and He will help us when we decide to go in a different direction. *Dear God, please forgive me. I have sinned with my body...*

_____
_____
_____
_____

*I want to use my whole body as an instrument to do what is right for your glory. Amen.*

Day 12

## Skinside: Heaven Says

The human body is one of the most incredible things created. If you know anything about anatomy and physiology, you can't deny there is a mastermind who created it. It is complex, integrated, and when it's working right, it is amazing!

> *Today you are You, that is truer than true.*
> *There is no one alive who is Youer than You.*
> — *Dr. Seuss*

Each person is uniquely made—a one of a kind. There is no one like you. God made the human body to be able to reproduce itself but no two are exact replicas. There is a system that God put in place. Scientists have named it genetics. We inherit traits from our mother and our father. A miraculous molecule, called our DNA, has a coding from each parent. That determines our physical qualities.

The National Association of Anorexia Neuroses and Associated Disorders reports only 5 percent of American females naturally possess the body type portrayed in advertising. But we believe the subtle message that we must all measure up to those images in spite of our DNA.

It is important to realize that God made us all different rather than have a preoccupation with size and weight. But it is our responsibility to take care of the body that we have. It is our temporary house, the one we have while we navigate planet earth, so it must last a while. But in heaven, we will have a forever body. We don't know what that will look like so for now we will focus on what God has given us for this part of our journey.

**Your genetics include:**　　　　　　　　　　　**How you feel about it:**
　Height: _____　　　　　　_____
　Natural Hair color: _____　　　　_____
　Eye color: _____　　　　_____
　Skin color: _____　　　　_____
　Body frame (S, M, L): _____　　　　_____

It's important to accept the body you have been born with, but it is even more important to respect that body. Often we don't appreciate our body, rather we abuse it. Sometimes we are not considerate or thoughtful about the bodies God has given us. In respecting them, we should properly care for the body we have.

## Nutrition

Part of living in our modern world is the choices we face that satisfy and give pleasure to our soul. Food is part of that. It is a constant battle to do what's right rather than what's good when it comes to food choices.

Nutritionists agree we need a proper balance of vitamins, minerals, protein, fiber, and water for our bodies to function in the way they should. A wide variety of healthy-eating plans exist to guide our food choices. The main thing is, be aware of what you should be doing and choose something you can stick with. We're not talking dieting, we are talking about proper eating for proper functioning of your body.

If you don't know what you should be eating, then take some time to research it. Develop a healthy approach to eating. By doing so, you will show that you care about your body. Because we are unique, we may not all benefit from the same things. Ask God's help with your choices.

*My healthy eating approach includes:*

## Weight Control

It is also important to consume the right amount of calories for your lifestyle; otherwise, you won't have enough energy for daily activities or you will store calories as extra weight.

Each person's weight guideline varies by height and bone structure. We should stay within those guidelines or our health will suffer. Below is a guideline that insurance companies use for women.

| Height | Small Frame | Medium Frame | Large Frame |
|---|---|---|---|
| 4'10" | 102 – 111 | 109 – 121 | 118 – 131 |
| 4'11" | 103 – 113 | 111 – 123 | 120 – 134 |
| 5'0" | 104 – 115 | 113 – 129 | 125 – 140 |

| | | | |
|---|---|---|---|
| 5'1" | 106 – 118 | 115 – 132 | 128 – 143 |
| 5'2" | 108 – 121 | 118 – 132 | 128 – 143 |
| 5'3" | 111 – 124 | 121 – 135 | 131 – 147 |
| 5'4" | 114 – 127 | 124 – 138 | 134 – 151 |
| 5'5" | 117 – 130 | 127 – 141 | 137 – 155 |
| 5'6" | 120 – 133 | 130 – 144 | 140 – 159 |
| 5'7" | 123 – 136 | 133 – 147 | 143 – 163 |
| 5'8" | 126 – 139 | 136 – 150 | 146 – 167 |
| 5'9" | 129 – 142 | 139 – 153 | 149 – 170 |
| 5'10" | 132 – 145 | 142 – 156 | 152 – 173 |
| 5'11" | 135 – 148 | 145 – 159 | 155 – 176 |
| 6'0" | 138 – 151 | 148 – 162 | 158 – 179 |
| | | | |

These are guidelines. They are general and don't include things like muscle mass which weighs more than fat. Don't become a slave to these numbers, but keep them in mind when trying to achieve a proper body weight.

The rule of thumb when trying to lose weight is to burn more calories than you consume. All food intake is assigned a calorie quantity. All exercise burns calories. Stating it simply, eat the foods that have smaller calories, don't consume more than you burn, and exercise to burn off the extra.

The rule of thumb when trying to gain weight is to consume more calories than you burn. Be conscious of healthy choices with higher calories and don't overdo the exercise.

*My Height:* _____  *My Ideal Weight:* _____

*Date:* _____

## Exercise

Exercise is also important for your body to function properly. It doesn't need to be vigorous but it should be regular. Not only is it important for weight control, it is important for your overall health and well-being. Your heart, lungs, bones, muscle, mental health, moods, and more all benefit when you exercise.

Exercise is easy to include when you find something you love to do. There are all kinds of physical activities. If you're social, join a group activity, such as an exercise class or a group which enjoys a particular activity like bicycling or hiking. If you enjoy quiet activity, you can find DVDs and exercise at home. This may sound like common knowledge, but it requires thought, planning, and follow-through.

*My Exercise Plan:*
_____
_____
_____
_____
_____

## Rest

Take time to rest. Even God rests. He created the earth and everything in it in six days. On the seventh day, He rested. If God needs rest, then we need rest. In the fast-paced world we live in, it's hard to unplug. We are connected globally and while we sleep, part of the world is awake. Because of technology, we have access to a world that never shuts off. But we can control the off button.

Wellness experts agree that we need between seven and nine hours of uninterrupted sleep each night. Add to that God's command to rest one day out of seven. To deprive your body of sleep sets you up for all kinds of problems. If you get less than six hours of sleep a night, you're likely to experience some of these things:

- Decrease in alertness, causing you to not retain what you learn
- Negative effects on your health, in particular your heart, blood pressure, and diabetes
- May cause you to be more emotional and less rational
- Weight loss or weight gain
- Depression

Your body repairs itself while you sleep. If you don't protect your rest, you may get into a habit of not getting enough sleep. Losing one hour of sleep one night won't cause these things, but over time they might begin to show up.

Sleeping with your phone near you may interrupt your sleep. Alerts come as texts, messages, and mail. Your curiosity won't let you rest. Sometimes that leads to extended sleep loss. Besides that, cell phones pump out electromagnetic radiation. Who wants to be exposed to that? Try leaving it in a nearby room, close enough for an emergency, but not close enough to be tempted to lose sleep.

Sometimes we just can't turn off our mind. So much happens at such a fast pace that we don't have time to process it or make decisions during the day. When we get still and are alone, usually at night, we will think things over. That can also cause sleep loss. Here are a few suggestions:

- Establish regular sleeping hours
- Don't eat or drink too close to bedtime or your body will keep you awake digesting
- If you have a lot to do the next day, make a list so thinking about the things you need to do won't keep you awake
- If you are worried about something, pray
- If you are angry, forgive
- If there is something you're thinking through, journal

*My Commitment to Rest:*

Daily: _____
_____
_____

Weekly: _____
_____
_____

## Cleanliness and Sanitation

Even in the Old Testament, God provided guidelines for avoiding sickness and disease. There were no emergency clinics, doctor's offices, or hospitals. God gave specific instructions in order that His people stay healthy. (You can read about them in the Bible, in the book of Leviticus.) It is important to know that we can prevent some sicknesses and diseases when we adopt certain practices in:

- Cleanliness (good grooming and personal hygiene)
- Sanitation (prevention of sickness)

Taking measures to keep yourself, your personal items, and your surroundings clean will help protect your health. Pathogens and microorganisms that cause disease breed in unsanitary environments. Avoiding unsanitary conditions through cleanliness is our responsibility.

## Fashion Guidelines

Fashion is and always has been an issue for women. Even in the New Testament, Paul gave instructions for how women should dress. Depending on the circle you travel in, you will adopt a certain style. Fashion is fun and what we choose to wear is an expression of our personality.

The temple that Solomon built as God's house was one of the most beautifully adorned structures ever built. The main thing to remember when choosing our fashion statement is that our body is a shared house with God. How would you decorate the temple of your body for God? Things to keep in mind are:

- Modesty
- Not to focus attention on our bodies but to the God of our bodies.
- Not to underplay or overplay the statement we make with our bodies.

*My Fashion Statement:*

Day 13

## Your Skinside

In changing your identity, the first step is changing the way you view your body. According to the scriptures, when we belong to God, so does our body. That's how God moves about on the earth–in us.

> Don't you know that you yourselves are God's temple
> and that God's Spirit dwells in you?
>
> —1 Cr. 3:16 NIV
>
> Don't you realize that your body is a temple of the Holy Spirit,
> who lives in you, and was given to you by God:
> You do not belong to yourself, for God bought you with a high price.
> So you must honor God with your body.
>
> —1Cr. 6:19–20 NLT

For most of us, that is a tough concept. We have always thought of our bodies as our own. But part of serving God is giving Him permission to indwell our bodies. Then we become partners with Him on the earth. The above scripture states that God gave us these bodies in the first place.

It's like someone gives you a new car and says you can use it as long as he can ride too. You decide you won't let them drive, or for that matter, you won't even ask them where they would like to go. You completely take over the car. While he is riding with you, you let the trash pile up inside of it. You don't wash it, never vacuum it, get into a wreck, and don't fix the dent. You might even break laws, or show off by drag racing, tempting fate. All the while, the giver is wondering why he's given you such a gift. He feels you don't respect it, or even like the gift he's given you. Wouldn't you wonder if you were the giver?

God has given each of us a body. We didn't get to choose it. It is a gift. Our gift varies. But the reason doesn't vary. A favorite movie from years ago was a true story of an Olympic runner, Eric Liddell, who claimed to feel God's presence when he ran. He was a devout Christian, born to missionary parents. He used his running and his body to glorify God. He got attention because of his speed but when he spoke, it was filled with his Christian beliefs. He is quoted in the movie, "I believe that God made me for a purpose. But he also made me fast, and when I run, I feel his pleasure." He believed that not to run would dishonor God.

There are ways in which we can honor God with our bodies. We can recognize the strengths he gives. Sometimes we must overcome adversity in order to glorify Him. But when we have such a preoccupation with our image because of Hollywood, it's hard to consider what God thinks. We are bombarded with the message that the media sends—that is, to have value, we must measure up to their ideal.

In reality, Hollywood is perfected with makeup, lighting, airbrushing, editing, right camera angles, and other such things. We love to see the smut magazines expose celebrities without their makeup or mascara. It gives us hope that ordinary people have value.

With God, everyone has value. It doesn't depend solely on our outward appearance. But He does expect us to respect our body. It will require us to use our bodies as instruments of righteousness rather than instruments of pleasure. Our culture has been dominated with the message of "if it feels good, do it". There might be some changes you need to make in your attitude toward your body.

Sometimes, that is easier said than done. It's a simple concept but disciplining ourselves is the tough part. Our old way of thinking and our habits are deep in our subconscious mind. In order to make changes, we will need to be intentional in thinking about things differently. When changing our direction and habits in life, these are steps to keep in mind.

*Seven Ds to Changing Your Subconscious Mind (Based on Changing Your Subconscious Mind by Creflo Dollar)*

1. **Decide** *you are going to change*
2. **Desire** *to change (you've got to want to)*
3. **Deepen** *your understanding through knowledge*
4. **Diligence** *– keep at it*
5. **Defend** *yourself against your old way of thinking*
6. **Disassociate** *with some people or circumstances*
7. **Depend** *on God to help you*

## Temporary Houses

We measure each other in superficial ways, or on the surface. We measure each other by the way things look. God measures us in ways that are more significant. He measures us by our character, by the things that are on the inside of each of us. That makes sense, because the body is only temporary, but the soul and spirit live on in the afterlife. That is the part of us that goes to live with God. Like Jesus, we will shed our body when we leave earth.

## Journal Time

Record your thoughts about your Skinside.

_____
_____
_____
_____
_____
_____ Date

*Day 14*

# Inside: Your Soul

## Personality of the Soul

The body is the temporary part of you, or your shell. But the soul is the forever part of you, the inside part—the real you—where you express your choices to the world. Inside of you is where your personality is formed.

Your personality is the total of the qualities and traits of your character and behavior. Your gifts and talents, your likes and dislikes, all of the things that are unique to you as an individual are a part of your soul. God wired you a certain way. The things that influence your personality are inherited, environmental, and innate, or they exist since birth.

The soul is the most powerful part of you. In the depth of your soul lies the map to your course in life. This is where you choose the path you will take to who and what you will become. It is also the most complex part of you. Understanding it takes time. It is important to begin to know yourself and to discover why you make certain choices. For more information on knowing how you are wired, read the book or take an online personality quiz: *Personality Plus* by Florence Littauer.

## Influences on Our Soul

We continually receive messages in our subconscious mind telling us who we should be. Visual and verbal messages bombard us from magazines, TV, and music. They tell us who we should be in subtle ways by presenting a desirable or undesirable message. Not only do we get pressure from those things, in addition, parents expect one thing while friends expect another thing, yet teachers and bosses expect something else. While listening to all these messages, you decide who you will become and exactly who you want to be, even if you don't know you're doing it.

But who will you listen to and who knows what is best for you? Oh, you may say, "If I don't like being this way, then I will change and be another way." Or, you may be one way with one set of people, and then when you're with another group, you will act a completely different way.

It's not easy to keep changing who you are. When you decide to change who you are, it will confuse everyone around you, and it will confuse you, too. Then you will become the many messages that you are hearing and seeing. Like flipping a switch, you turn into another personality, depending upon the moment. But you can decide who you are and stick with it.

In your soul is where character is developed. We find the character traits of a Christian in the Bible. We find the character traits of Hollywood in the media. If you want to discover the character traits of being a Christian, it's necessary to read the Bible and hang out with others who exemplify Christian traits. If you don't put forth the effort to know the expectations of God then you will be subject to the expectations of Hollywood or to those you hang out with.

## Soul Is: Emotions, Mind, and Will

Within our soul is our personality. It helps to think of personality as three parts—emotion, mind, and will. Each has a part to play in projecting what's on the inside.

## Emotion

Emotions are a response to what's happening inside. Circumstances and other stimulus will trigger an emotion. Information from the outside is taken in through our five senses: sight, smell, hearing, touch, and taste. We respond to this communication with emotion. As babies, we communicate our feelings with emotion.

Feelings come from the inside, such as sad, happy, afraid, excited, angry, or tender. Those feelings trigger a corresponding emotion such as crying, laughing, yelling, sulking, or loving. Our emotions alert us to what's going on, even when we don't understand. By taking time to understand our emotional reaction with our mind, we will know ourselves better. If we live our lives based only on emotion, we will likely not reach our potential. Part of maturity is learning to control the reactions of our emotions through understanding them in our mind.

## Mind

Our mind is where we process information and determine priorities. When we haven't determined our priorities, our choices will reflect that. Behavior will be unpredictable because emotions will determine choice. And emotions change on a regular basis.

The mind is the control center, or your hard drive. All information is stored in the mind. In today's culture, it's easy to be overloaded with information. We take in information, and in subtle ways, it influences decisions. Who hasn't googled something only to have it show up as a pop-up later? The same is true in our mind. When random thoughts occur, it's likely that we've been exposed to something similar in our past.

Thoughts prompt action. Therefore, what we allow into our minds molds our lives. Education, as an example, is mentally focusing on a specific subject in order to be effective in a particular field. As we read or see something, we agree with it mentally then duplicate it in our actions.

All information we receive is processed in the mind. And in the mind is the culmination of all our past experiences, including family influences from our DNA to our environment, education, and personal experiences from books to relationships with others. So it's important to guard your mind because what you let in influences you.

## Will

The will is the deciding part of you. This is where you make choices. When you decide something, you take a course of action, and through determination, you make it happen. On day 7, we discovered both the heart (emotion) and the brain (mind) are trying to determine our destiny. So how will you make decisions? Sometimes we follow the lives of those we envy. It could be famous people, celebrities, friends, or relatives. But ultimately, we all decide what we choose and how we live.

God knew we could learn how to live through the lives of other people. That was Jesus's purpose. He came to earth to be an example of how God wanted us to live our lives. "Oh, great!" you say. "I don't want to have to die on a cross!" But the example we should focus on is His resurrection. He went to heaven. He shed His body but His soul, connected to God's spirit, now lives forever. And we will too, by following the example of the life of Jesus.

# HEAVEN BOUND IN A HOLLYWOOD WORLD

Scientists have researched the mind extensively over the past few decades. Discoveries have been made showing the mind can be altered. But it takes a continual effort of putting things into the mind. If we want to change our soul to identify with Christian characteristics, it will be a continual effort. As we do, our will to follow through with positive actions becomes easier.

*Spend some time thinking about what influences your mind? You might consider how you spend most of your time. Doddle them in this box in order of the time you spend from the greatest to the least.*

If the things that influence you are causing you to make poor choices, consider changing how you spend your time.

I would like to change _____
to _____.

Day 15

## Inside: Hollywood Says

Hollywood presents everything from a fairy tale life to the ridiculous or stupid. Entertainment is the purpose, but it is the product of someone's imagination. But whose imagination? Those productions are considered an art form and the artist sends his personal message each time. Conflicting messages from each creator's mind in Hollywood could be the source of our confusion about what's good, evil, right, or wrong.

It's hard to believe we are influenced by what we let into our minds but psychologists agree. They say our influences affect our emotions and our emotions influence our body.

"I think you're addicted to drama."

"Well, who isn't these days?"

"Yeah, but you just keep falling into crap. It's gotta be taking a toll on your emotions. I mean, who could experience what you have and keep going."

"I just keep hoping it's gonna get better. It's got to. Losing my mom when I was twelve was bad enough. That broke my heart. I kept hoping my stepdad would like me but nothing I did made him happy. It even made him mad that I would cook mom's favorite dinner for him.

"Yeah, I remember when you came over to spend the night and you had that black eye."

"Thanks for not telling your mom. If he would have gone to jail, I wouldn't have had any place to live."

"No problem, but you could have lived with us."

"That's a nice idea, but I would have gone to DCS and we both know it."

"Then there was Benny. He was so funny. But it wasn't funny that he died."

"Yeah, cancer took away his humor for sure. No one should have cancer that young."

"So sad."

"He was the best boyfriend anybody could ever have. When he made me laugh, I could forget about my mom…and my stepdad."

"How about Kane. Boy, was he cute!"

"Yeah, I kinda got lost in his dreamy eyes. Lost myself totally, even my virginity."

"Did they ever find out if that guy in the red convertible came out of the coma?"

"Yeah, but they say he doesn't remember the wreck. Doesn't even remember he took someone's life because of his stupid behavior."

"Poor Kane."

"You mean, poor me. I'm the survivor. He's peaceful now. I still gotta live this crap life."

"Did you stop cutting, yet?"

"Yeah, for now."

"You're cuts have healed pretty good."

"Not good enough for me not to remember."

"Remember? What are you talking about?"

"That I cut just to feel something again."

"Did you?"

"Did I what?"

"Feel anything?"

"No. I was numb. Everywhere, even my body."

"Is that why you wrecked your car? To feel something?"

"No, it wasn't my fault."

"You're right. None of this has been your fault. It's all just happened. But why did you look away when you saw the driver's signal? You knew he was going to turn."

"I hated that song. It was Kane's and my favorite. I had to change it. I only looked away for a split second. Just a millisecond."

"But now look at you. Broken bones all over and maybe a brain injury. How do you feel now?"

"I'll feel better when Austin comes to see me."

"I thought you said you broke up?"

"He can't break up with me now. I need him. Emotional support."

"I thought you said he couldn't deal with your drama."

"He'll be here. I know he will. He said he loves me."

"Yeah, that only lasted 'til he slept with you."

"That's not fair. He's been really kind."

"Then where is he? You've been in the hospital for three days now."

"He had a race."

"So that's more important than you?"

"No, but he paid a lot to enter. He can't lose that. And he stands to win fifteen hundred dollars."

"So emotionally supporting the love of his life is worth less than fifteen hundred dollars?"

"Shut up! That's not fair."

"When are you gonna wake up? When are you gonna take charge of your life?"

"I can't help it. Bad things just keep happening to me."

"No, bad things just keep happening in your head. It's the way you see things. You knew your mom wouldn't last long doing those drugs. And really, you and Benny broke up a year before his cancer. And you only went out with Austin twice. You're making it seem like you're the only one who has bad things happen to them."

"But for real, bad things keep happening. I'm not making this up."

"But it's becoming a mountain. You'll never be able to climb this mountain. It's gonna crumble. You're gonna crumble. It's built on your emotions."

"I can't help how I feel. It sucks what's happened to me."

"Yeah, but this car wreck is different. Like I said, I think you're starting to be addicted to drama. You couldn't feel anything from cutting so you are getting an emotional high from this bad stuff. It keeps you going for a while, but pretty soon, you'll have to create some more drama."

"Someday, something good is gonna happen."

"But who will you have to share it with? You're starting to wear everyone out with your stories. How can anyone compete with all this drama?"

"Because when I find him, all of this will disappear. None of it will matter when I fall in love."

"So, you're looking for Prince Charming to rescue you?"

"Sure. Isn't that what happens?"

"Only in fairy tales. In real life, no one can erase what's happened. No person can rescue you from all the bad stuff. That is…no one around here."

"So…where is he then?"

"He's in heaven."

"Heaven?"

"Yeah, only God can heal a broken heart. Not Prince Charming. That's too big of a job. It takes the most powerful one to help in times like yours."

"I just have this feeling that someday it's all going to be okay and I'll be at peace."

"You can be at peace. That's what God offers. But you have to trust Him. You have to trust that despite all these bad things, He's got a plan and reasons for what happens to anyone who turns to Him for help. You gotta believe that He won't let you down just because others have."

This kind of drama can keep us from developing our personality. Our personality is the expression of who we are. When we perpetuate drama, we are expressing Hollywood. Sometimes it is an exaggeration of truth. By expressing drama, we forget to express who God made us. You are a lot more interesting than the drama. And you are unique in who you are. There is no one like you and no one has the same life as you. It's easy to get sucked into living a drama-filled life when we see so much around us. But it's also exhausting.

Emotions can lead us to God. In times when we don't understand our emotions, we can ask God's help. He made us and He knows us, and when we are quiet, we can hear from God. And we can build our priorities. We can choose what's important in our lives before our circumstances lead us astray.

*Journal Time:*
*What emotions are you struggling with?*
_____
_____
_____


*What's going on inside? (Take time to be quiet and think about this.)*
_____
_____
_____


*What other course of action could you take? (Ask God's help.)*
_____
_____
_____


*Spend some time talking to God about this.*

Day 16

## Inside: Heaven Says

We are created by God. We are all wired in a certain way. He uses our DNA coding, the environment we are born into, and special things we are born with. Those are God-given gifts and talents. We discover these things while living our lives.

God also knows we will act like those around us. Whether you fill your mind with things that create godly character or whether you fill your mind with things that create a selfish character is up to you. Your choice lies in your will.

> Watch what God does, and then you do it, like children who learn proper behavior from their parents. Mostly what God does is love you. Keep company with him and learn a life of love. Observe how Christ loved us. His love was not cautious but extravagant. He didn't love in order to get something from us but to give everything of himself to us. Love like that.
>
> Don't allow love to turn into lust, setting off a downhill slide into sexual promiscuity, filthy practices, or bullying greed. Though some tongues just love the taste of gossip, Christians have better uses for language than that. Don't talk dirty or silly. That kind of talk doesn't fit our style. Thanksgiving is our dialect.
>
> You can be sure that using people or religion or things just for what you can get out of them - the usual variations on idolatry – will get you nowhere, and certainly nowhere near the kingdom of Christ, the kingdom of God.
>
> Don't let yourselves get taken in by religious smooth talk. God gets furious with people who are full of religious sales talk but want nothing to do with him. Don't even hang around people like that.

> You groped your way through that murk once, but no longer. You're out in the open now. The bright light of Christ makes your way plain. So no more stumbling around. Get on with it! The good, the right, the true – these are the actions appropriate for daylight hours. Figure out what will please Christ, and then do it……….
>
> Don't live carelessly, unthinkingly. Make sure you understand what the Master wants.
>
> —Ephesians 5: 1–13, 17 MSG

When you decide, in your mind, to make godly living a priority in your life, you will begin to have a plan and goals. You will begin to use more than your emotions to guide you. You will be able to prioritize the things that are important in your thoughts, and then in your behavior.

Learning to accept the life that God has given us will eliminate a lot of anger, frustration, and drama. The things we can't control in our lives are often what God uses to strengthen us. When we accept God's spirit into our lives, we should trust that He's using even the bad things for His plan in our lives. This will help us spend energy on what's important, not on what we can't change.

> **And we know that God causes everything to work together for the good of those who love God and are called according to his purpose for them.**
>
> —Rom. 8:28 NLT

Notice the scripture says that God has a purpose for us. It says He calls us. We are the ones who respond to His call. But usually when He calls us, we have already had some bad things happen in our lives. The scripture doesn't say these things happen in our lives because God decided they *should* happen. It doesn't say He made them happen. We have a free will. We do the choosing in our circumstances. The scripture says He will cause all of those things to "work together" for our good as long as we love God and are choosing to follow Him.

When we are following God, we will make better choices. We will begin to develop priorities. Reading the Bible will help us establish the order of importance in our lives. Jesus Himself gave a talk about establishing what should be the most important thing in our lives.

> "If you decide for God, living a life of God-worship, it follows that you don't fuss about what's on the table at mealtimes or whether the clothes in your closet are in fashion. There is far more to your life than the food you put in your stomach, more to your outer appearance than the clothes you hang on your body. Look at the birds, free and unfettered, not tied down to a job description, careless in the care of God. And you count far more to him than birds."
>
> "Has anyone by fussing in front of the mirror ever gotten taller by so much as an inch? All this time and money washed on fashion – do you think it makes that much difference? Instead of looking at the fashions, walk out into the fields and look at the wildflowers. They never primp or shop, but have you ever seen color and design quite like it? The ten best-dressed men and women in the country look shabby alongside them."
>
> "If God gives such attention to the appearance of wildflowers – most of which are never even seen – don't you think he'll attend to you, take pride in you, do his best for you? What I'm trying to do here is to get you to relax, to not be so preoccupied with getting, so you can respond to God's giving. People who don't know God and the way he works fuss over these things, but you know both God and how he works. Steep your life in God-reality, God-initiative, God-provisions. Don't worry about missing out. You'll find all your everyday human concerns will be met."
>
> —Matthew 6: 25–32 MSG

Don't misunderstand what this is saying. It is not saying don't work, don't think about eating or shopping. It says to get your priorities right. The things of God should be first, what He's doing in your life and in the lives of others. The Bible says to not be preoccupied with the things that don't really matter. The things of godly living should be our number one priority.

*Dear God,*

*Help me establish my priorities. Help me spend time on things that will last forever.*

_____
_____
_____
_____
_____
_____
_____
_____
_____ *Amen.*

Day 17

## Your Inside

It is the most important part of us. It includes our emotions, mind, and will, which is our personality. But the most important part of our inside (our soul) is the power of choice. God gave us a free will because it's important that we choose to follow Him and not be slaves. Otherwise, we could not freely express Him with our personalities in the world.

When we invite God to live inside us, we will have a God-conscious. We will be aware of the things in our lives that are taking us away from living a God-centered life. We will sense when we are going in a wrong direction. But it is up to us to go in the direction He is leading us.

We may know, in our mind, what we should do in a particular situation, but the action or the willpower to do something is up to us. God doesn't control us like a robot. But he will help us go in the right direction when we make up our minds. He will either strengthen our willpower or He will rearrange the circumstances. He wants to help us.

As adults, we should never give the power of choice for our lives to someone else, especially to Hollywood. Drama comes out of Hollywood and is based on a pretend reality. A drama is a screenplay or theatrical event but it also has another meaning. It is a situation or series events in real life that has a progression of dramatic events that lead to emotional effect. Such is the case of the girl from day15.

So how can we untangle the mess of continuing drama? The Bible gives a solution.

> ...then take on an entirely new way of life – a God-fashioned life,
> a life renewed from the inside and working itself into your conduct
> as God accurately reproduces his character in you.
>
> What this adds up to, then, is this: no more lies, no more pretense.
> Tell your neighbor the truth.
>
> —Ephesians 4:22b–25a MSG

Inside the soul is where you really decide how to live life. This part of you has the ability to make choices and truth should rule. This is where thoughts occur and thoughts guide actions.

Sometimes, we need help in understanding ourselves. We are complex. We need to talk to someone. It may be a friend, a pastor, a mentor, or a counselor. They will help. But sometimes all we need to do is stop our actions, think about what's driving our decisions, and get control.

Our emotions show what's going on inside, our mind processes information based on past exposure, but our will determines our course of action. When you can't get a handle on your emotions, or your emotional state is prolonged, it may be a sign that something is wrong in your body. It could be that your hormone or brain chemistry is out of balance. In that case, a doctor's advice is necessary.

Choosing to follow God's way will help us develop a behavior that's pleasing to God. It's less confusing than following Hollywood. The Bible never changes. God never changes. He is the same yesterday, today, and forever. His ways don't depend on changing culture because His ways deal with character. Character is something we can train within ourselves. But we can create a filter that every decision goes through by adopting the truth in the Bible as our guide.

*Over the following week, take the time to notice your emotional responses to circumstances or other stimulus. Record them.*

_____
_____
_____

*What triggered these emotions? (Understand them with your mind.)*

_____
_____
_____

*Determine your path by choosing how to handle your emotions.*

- *I have the courage to change my circumstances. God, please help me take the necessary steps.*
- *I accept that I cannot change these circumstances. Please give me peace about it, God.*
- *Help me God, know what I need courage for and what I need peace in.*

*A Famous Prayer by: Reinhold Niebuhr*
*Known as "The Serenity Prayer"*

God, give me grace to accept with serenity
the things that cannot be changed,
Courage to change the things
which should be changed,
and the Wisdom to distinguish
the one from the other.

Living one day at a time,
Enjoying one moment at a time,

Accepting hardship as a pathway to peace,
Taking, as Jesus did,
This sinful world as it is,
Not as I would have it,
Trusting that You will make all things right,
If I surrender to Your will,
So that I may be reasonably happy in this life,
And supremely happy with You forever in the next.

Amen

Day 18

# Deeperside: The Spirit

## Spirit World

Another dimension exists besides the world we live in. We know because we read about it in the Bible. That other dimension is the spirit world. When God created this world, He had already been in existence. God has the quality of being infinite. That means without time or boundaries. The world that we are confined to is limited by time and it has boundaries. But God's world isn't.

As Christians, the Bible promises a place in the spirit world, living with God, forever in heaven. We won't live in the bodies we have now. They have an expiration date. It's called death. Our bodies will come to an end. But since God's world doesn't have an end, our spirits don't have an end when our bodies cease to exist. Our spirit is the part of us that will exist with God forever.

But as humans, we exist in a world that is finite. That means it has time and boundaries. We exist in the boundary of our body for a limited period of time. We might daydream or imagine we are in another place but our body has limitations. We can only be in one place at one time.

God doesn't have those limitations. He exists everywhere at the same time. That's why God is the same yesterday, today, and forever. He never changes. Circumstances don't sway who He is. They do, however, sway who we are.

The challenge, when considering things of the spirit world, is to develop who we are on the inside into the never changing, never swayed by circumstances, character of God. When we seek to understand that, it will help us understand how to navigate our ever changing circumstances in this world.

## Jesus Promised

Jesus came into the world to be an example of how we can live in this world, having a positive effect on others as we keep our eyes on God's kingdom of heaven. He wants us to travel through this life, keeping focused on Him and the promised eternal life, and not be distracted by the selfish pleasures offered in this world. When we keep our attention on God's ways, He will guide us this life. Our circumstances should bring us into His presence as we ask what His will is for us on this earth.

Jesus came to show us the way to God. He taught us how to think differently than the world thinks. In the world, we are taught to think about ourselves, how to get what we want—love, money, success, and significance—based on what people think of us. But Jesus taught us how to get significance based on what God thinks of us. When focusing on God's love and acceptance, we learn to trust what He has in store for us.

> **...and anyone who looks up to him [Jesus], trusting and expectant, will gain a real life, eternal life.**
>
> "This is how much God loved the world; He gave his Son, his one and only Son. And this is why;
>
> so that no one need be destroyed; by believing in him, anyone can have a whole and lasting life.
>
> God didn't go to all the trouble of sending his Son merely to point an accusing finger, telling the world how bad it was. He came to help, to put the world right again.
>
> Anyone who trusts in him is acquitted; anyone who refuses to trust him has long since been under the death sentence without knowing it. And why? Because of that person's failure to believe him, the one-of-a-kind Son of God, when introduced to him.
>
> "This is the crisis we're in: God-light streamed into the world, but men and women everywhere ran for the darkness.

> They went for darkness because they were not really interested in pleasing God.
>
> Everyone who makes a practice of doing evil, addicted to denial and illusion, hates God-light and won't come near it, fearing a painful exposure. But anyone working and living in truth and reality welcomes God-light so the work can be seen for the God-work it is."
>
> —John 3: 15a–21 MSG

## Enemies of the Spirit

In every story and every circumstance of life, there are enemies. An enemy is an opposing force. We even see it in natural things: what goes up must come down or for every action, there is a reaction. Nothing goes unopposed. But for some reason, humans don't expect opposition, especially when we consider ourselves Christians. We believe our life should go unopposed and God will make sure of it. Or that He should grant us our every wish. That kind of thinking belongs in fairy tales: genie in a bottle, the fairy godmother, Santa Clause, and such. But in reality, there is always an enemy, especially in God's kingdom because our eternal destiny is at stake.

Jesus gave this enemy a name. He is Satan and often referred to as the devil. He also has a kingdom in the spirit world. He has authority over certain activity. He also has demons at his command, like God has angels at his command. But when we become followers of God, Satan does not have authority over us. He may try intimidation, but as citizens of God's kingdom, we are under God's protection.

But sometimes we wander from God's kingdom. Then we take ourselves out of his protection. When we go places where Satan has authority, we are subject to him and his influences, even as Christians.

*Take some time to consider three things:*

1. *What is keeping me from conforming to Godly character?*

2. *What earthly pleasure is keeping me from trusting God's best for me?*

3. *Have I taken myself out of God's protection?*

Day 19

## Deeperside: Hollywood Says

### In the Movies

Over the years, there have been lots of movies about the spirit world. Hollywood must agree there is another realm besides the one we see with our eyes and experience with our five senses. What Hollywood says doesn't often agree with what the Bible says. But remember, what comes out of Hollywood is the product of the producer's imagination. Most do not create movies based on biblical truth but based on their own thoughts.

Some movies about the spirit world include hopeful situations, like reuniting with a loved one, or being granted a second chance at life, or having a positive effect on those previously known. With these kinds of movies, you get a mixed bag of nuts as to what the next life might be like, but most of these movies give hope of circumstances that may need to be changed or made right.

There are also movies that portray the next life as demonic. A lot of scary movies portray the dead coming back to this life to haunt or hunt others. These movies are based on fear. By stimulating this emotion, the producers desire to make lots of money. And it's true, our emotions give us an adrenaline rush. And we like the feeling of our heart beating faster, maybe our palms sweating, as the hormone, adrenaline, is released into our body.

Hollywood makes movies that stir emotions because they know that's why we watch them. Hollywood's goal is to make money, not tell the truth. If we don't know truth, we may ponder or consider their content as truth. They can affect the way we think about the spirit world.

## The Biggest Lie

Most will believe the lie; that this life, what we can get while we are here, is all there is and then the end comes. But at some point in everyone's life, the question will arise on the inside; why am I here? What is my purpose? To add to that, why are there so many struggles? If God controls the whole world then why is it so bad? Why do little children die, why are the innocent murdered, and why won't someone love me for who I am? These are all questions that don't seem to have answers.

To some, it means that God doesn't exist. They may think; if he exists, he wouldn't allow such things, or He isn't giving me what I want so there must not be a God. Let's go back to something we already covered. In day 3, we discovered that we have been captured by the enemy and are living in his kingdom. In other words, humanity has come under his control. He won us over with lies. And the lies didn't stop with Eve and Adam in the garden of paradise. They continue every day—in the media, in our minds, and in the majority of those presently living on earth. It's like living under enemy attack every day. Before long, we believe those lies as truth.

## The Spirit of Truth

Existing in God's spirit world means living in truth. If there is an opposing force against truth, it is lies. And a lie is a false truth. If I wanted to imitate something to cause someone to believe it was authentic, I would come as close to the original as possible. Satan presents his lies in the same way.

> And no marvel; for Satan himself is transformed into an angel of light.
>
> —2 Cor. 11:14, KJV

Satan's biggest influencer is appealing to our desires, comfort, and convenience. He causes us to believe we can have, should have, and will have all the things we desire. Our culture is built on these lies because just like the Hollywood movies, it appeals to our emotions.

It's not wrong to want and have things in this life. They bring us pleasure, and we should give praise to God for His provisions. But sometimes, they get in the way of developing godly character. Just like the adrenaline rush in scary movies, we can get an adrenaline rush when we pursue one thing after another in life. When achieving those things becomes our focus, it will take our attention away from developing a godly character. They can get in the way of knowing what our purpose is and what God's plans are.

## The Purpose of Lies

Satan has a purpose, just like *we* have a purpose. Jesus is our example in all things. Satan tempted Him to give up heaven for what he could have in this life. We are no different. If Satan tempted Jesus, he will tempt us. The temptation is to give up the promise of heaven and eternity for the pleasures and satisfaction we can gain on earth. Satan tempts with lies. The opposing force is God's truth. See how Jesus handled Satan's temptation.

> Then Jesus was led by the Spirit into the desert to be tempted by the devil. After fasting forty days and forty nights, he was hungry. The tempter came to him and said, "If you are the Son of God, tell these stones to become bread."
>
> Jesus answered, "It is written: 'Man does not live on bread alone, but on every word that comes from the mouth of God.'"
>
> Then the devil took him to the holy city and had him stand on the highest point of the temple. "If you are the Son of God," he said, "throw yourself down, For it is written: "He will command his angels concerning you, and they will lift you up in their hands, so that you will not strike your foot against a stone."
>
> Jesus answered him, "It is also written: 'Do not put the Lord your God to the test.'"
>
> Again, the devil took him to a very high mountain and showed him all the kingdoms of the world and their splendor. "All this I will give you," he said, "if you will bow down and worship me."
>
> "Jesus said to him, "Away from me, Satan! For it is written, "Worship the Lord your God, and serve him only."
>
> Then the devil left him and angels came and attended him.
>
> —Matthew 4: 1–11 NIV

## Our Temptation

If Jesus was tempted, then we will surely be tempted. List some of the ways you feel you are tempted to trade godly character for pleasure, satisfaction, or achievement:

_____
_____
_____
_____
_____
_____
_____

Ask God to show you His truth and Satan's lies. Be quiet and listen for His answer in your spirit.

Day 20

# Deeperside: Heaven Says

God knows our weaknesses and our temptations. Not only because He created us but also because He came to live among us as a human in the person of Jesus. He faced temptation and trial just as we do. But He kept God's ways first in His life. He taught His disciples and others how to do the same. He taught them how to know God personally, as He lived among them.

This circle of friends helped Him influence the world with God's message. As long as He was with them, they were able to keep His message in their hearts. But when He left earth, they became weak and discouraged. They didn't have that constant reminder as when He walked and talked with them daily. You know the saying, "out of sight, out of mind.". That's how the disciples were. When Jesus was sentenced to death, they were confused.

God knew His daily presence with us would be important in order for us to keep strong in following His ways. So He gave us a helper. He gave us a piece of Himself called the Holy Spirit. God's spirit lives within all of us who invite Him in. This is the constant reminder that he is with us in every circumstance and we can choose godly character over cultural standards. Knowing God is with us keeps us strong.

"This piece of crap I'm driving has become a blessing."

"I would think it's been a curse and not a blessing."

"Yeah, you would think. But ever since I heard the pastor give a message about the opportunity God gives us in our circumstances, I've changed my mind."

"What's that mean?"

"Well, he said when you follow God's ways to the best of your ability, every circumstance in your life has a purpose."

"I don't see how that's possible. That rust bucket has spent a lot of time in mechanic and body shops. How is that good and what's the purpose in that?"

"When I changed the way I looked at things, it made sense. I used to think like you, too. But the pastor told us if we look for God, then we will see Him."

"So, what? Was he in your backseat?"

"No, silly. I found Him in the middle of my circumstances. I started asking Him to show up and show me how to look at my car in a different way."

"So, did he?"

"Yep, just like the pastor said. The first time was when my fuel pump went out."

"So then you prayed and you didn't need a fuel pump?"

"No, I needed the fuel pump. It's like the heart of your car. It pumps the go-juice. At least that's what the mechanic said."

"Pumps the go-juice?"

"Yeah. My car just quit running. I was on my way home from work and it quit running…right in front of a mechanic shop. So I walked over and talked to this guy about fixing it."

"And did he?"

"Sure. He knew how. But as I was walking over to his shop, I asked God to show me how this part of my journey had a purpose."

"Did he answer you?"

"Yeah, but not like I thought he would. I thought I would get a miracle and maybe it wouldn't cost me anything. But it did."

"What's good about that?"

"Well, here's what happened. When I walked into the mechanic shop, I could tell he was a troubled man. At first, I wasn't sure I could trust him, but I was committed to trusting God in my circumstances. Turned out he was an ace mechanic…and his price was fair."

"So, end of story?"

"Not quite. I haven't gotten to the good part yet. When I picked up my car, I thanked him. That's when he said the fuel pump was like the heart of a car. Then a thought came to me and I decided to be bold and say it out loud. I said, 'Just like you fixed the heart of my car, God can fix your heart.'"

"No, way! You said that? Was it awkward?"

"Yeah, for about a split second. Then I saw a tear roll down his cheek. He turned away and fiddled with my bill. Then he turned back around and smiled. He said thanks and handed me my keys and his business card."

"Then what happened?"

"The next time my car needed something, I called him. I had to have it towed to his place. That cost a little extra, but I got a raise the next week at work so in four weeks I had it covered. Then I got to enjoy the raise."

"What did it need this time, a liver?"

"How'd you guess? The mechanic said it was sort of like a liver. Turns out there was gunk in my oil filter. Oil makes the engine run smoothly, but when it gets gunked up, the engine won't run like it should."

"This guy sounds like the car doctor."

"That's funny, 'cause that's the name of his shop, The Car Doctor."

"Did you get a miracle this time? Like he didn't charge you or you miraculously didn't need an oil filter or whatever he did?

"No. The way you're thinking takes us out of our circumstances with a miracle. Sort of like we're rescued. But he uses our circumstances, not eliminate them. He uses our circumstances to create a miracle."

"What? You're talking riddles."

"This time when I paid the bill, which once again, the raise covered in two weeks plus a week for the tow, he said, 'The filter is like our liver. And the filter takes care of all the junk so our engine can run properly.' I had another thought and said it out loud again. I said, 'God's word, the Bible, is our life filter. It helps filter out all the junk so we can live properly.'"

"Man! He must think you're a kook."

"It didn't matter to me what he thought. I figured he was getting what he wanted. He was making a living by fixing my car. So, why shouldn't God get what he wanted, someone to tell him that God could make a difference in his life.

"So what happened?"

"I invited him to church."

"Did he come?"

"Not at first. But after two more times to his shop for him to fix my car, he finally agreed to come. He was baptized last week after coming for a while, and he gave his testimony in front of everyone."

"What was his testimony?"

"Seems like he felt screwed by everybody. He lost a child at age five in a car wreck. Five years later, his wife left him because she couldn't handle the death of their child. I guess she went a little crazy 'cause she was driving the day of the wreck. He decided to fill up his time with work. So he and a partner opened The Car Doctor. Four years into it, his partner stole all the money and left town. He lost his house, his car, and most of his stuff. He had to move into an apartment. He was getting pretty bitter by then. But he kept going to work. He kinda buried himself in it. Then after he started going to church, he met people who cared about him and showed him the importance forgiving the people who screwed him. He said he has a fresh start now, and he feels like he can live for the first time."

"Did he mention you in his testimony?"

"No. He didn't need to."

"It would have been nice to get a little credit."

"I got all the credit I need. I know God is pleased. And here is the miracle. That guy's life is changed forever."

"Wow, that's some story."

"So now do you see how the crappy car is a blessing?"

"Yep, I see. And you're right, it depends on how you look at it."

When we give God permission to come live inside of us, then His spirit or taking on His nature becomes our priority. Our spirit is then the central nature of who we are. We use our emotion, mind, and will to get to know God and understand His nature. As we are united in spirit, His will becomes our will.

But the world we experience every day is guiding our emotions, mind, and will. It takes a concentrated effort to get to know God and what His will is, especially in the midst of our circumstances. The world is filled with visual and verbal messages that drive our priorities and they are usually selfish. The way to get to know God is in solitude.

Our body needs care, our soul needs care, and our spirit needs care, too. We eat, sleep, shop, and go to concerts. Those are needs and wants of the body and the soul. Sometimes, as Christians, we forget the needs of the spirit. Not taking time alone with God is like starving the Spirit inside.

*How do I look at the circumstances in my life; blessings or curses?*

*Are my priorities self-focused; are they based on my pleasure, my comfort, or convenience?*

*Do I want God's will to become a priority in my life; based on pleasing Him?*

*Has God's will become my will?*

*How much time do I spend getting to know God?*

*What am I willing to do in order for that to happen?*

*Have I asked for the Holy Spirit's help?*

## Day 21

# Your Deeperside

As we invite God into our lives, His spirit comes alive in us. But not until we give Him permission to have His way in us. We are born with natural desires and our culture provides plenty to want or to be involved with that lead us away from God. Eliminating distractions becomes a full-time management job.

But the Holy Spirit, God's spirit that was alive in Jesus, helps us with priorities. The Holy Spirit was contained in Jesus when He was alive on earth. When Jesus entered into eternity with God, a miracle occurred. He had no boundaries, and His spirit could live in each of us at the same time.

## The Promise of the Holy Spirit

Jesus talked to His disciples about this promise of the Holy Spirit before His death. He told them the Holy Spirit would have three purposes.

1. Convince the world of its sin
2. Convince the world of God's goodness
3. Convince the world it can be delivered from judgment

> "But now I am going away to the one who sent me;
> and none of you seems interested in the purpose of my going; none wonders why.
>
> Instead, you are only filled with sorrow.
>
> But the fact of the matter is that it is best for you that I go away,
> for if I don't, the Comforter won't come.
>
> If I do, he will – for I will send him to you.
>
> And when he has come he will
> convince the world of its sin,
> and of the availability of God's goodness,
> and of deliverance from judgment."
>
> —John 16: 5–8 TLB

**The First Purpose of the Holy Spirit**

The first purpose of the Holy Spirit is to convince the world of sin. Jesus went on to explain what sin is to His disciples. "The world's sin is unbelief in me" (John 16:9).

If you try to believe with your mind that God came to earth and limited Himself to the finite world in the body of Jesus, you'll find it's impossible. It doesn't make sense. We can't prove it because it only happened one time. But belief in God is the foundation of Christianity. Remember, if we could explain God, then we would be God. It takes faith.

Faith is something we can't see or prove. It is also more than hope or belief. Its confidence and certainty in what cannot be proven. This quote from footnotes in the *Life Application Bible* explains it well:

> Two words describe our faith; confidence and certainty. These two qualities need a secure beginning and ending point. The beginning point of faith is believing in God's character—He is who He says. The end point is believing in God's promises—He will do what He says. We believe

that God will fulfill His promises even though we don't see those promises materializing now—this is true faith.

—Heb.11:1, *Life Application Bible: The Living Bible*, page 1908, Tyndale, 1988

## The Second Purpose of the Holy Spirit

The second purpose of the Holy Spirit is to convince the world of God's goodness. When we look at nature, we see His goodness; when we look at tragedy, we question God's goodness. We need the Holy Spirit to help us see things like God does. Sometimes our definition of goodness isn't God's definition of goodness.

There is another word used for goodness. It is righteousness. That means what is right in God's eyes, or what is good in God's eyes. We sometimes justify and excuse things in the world or in our lives that aren't right in God's eyes. But heaven is His kingdom and He is the one who should say what's right and what's good, not us. Otherwise, we will live in our own kingdom, not His.

The Holy Spirit lives within us to help us think of the world differently. It helps us to know God's righteousness and goodness. We can ask for His help when we don't understand things. We also have the Bible to confirm God's ways. There are many stories about things that went wrong but turned out right. The story of Joseph in Genesis 37–50 is one of the most famous. His brothers sold him into slavery, but he ended up ruling a nation and saving their lives.

Sometimes we have to wait for righteousness and goodness to be revealed. Judging too quickly in a situation usually means we are stating our opinion. Instead, we should pray for the situation while we wait for goodness and allow the Holy Spirit to help us think God's way.

## The Third Purpose of the Holy Spirit

The third purpose of the Holy Spirit is to deliver us from judgment by showing us truth. When we follow the ways of Satan's kingdom, we receive the same judgment he receives. When we follow the ways of God's kingdom, we are delivered from this judgment.

Jesus came into the world to make the world right with God, like it was in the beginning with Adam and Eve. God gave the Holy Spirit so we could have help seeing things the way He sees them. Satan is a deceiver and twists truth to suit him. He deceived Adam and Eve and is still doing the same thing. The Bible says this:

> "If our Message is obscure to anyone, it's not because we're holding back in any way. No, it's because these other people are looking or going the wrong way and refuse to give it serious attention. All they have eyes for is the fashionable god of darkness. They think he can give them what they want, and that they won't have to bother believing a Truth they can't see."
>
> —2 Cor. 4: 3–5 MSG

God is the creator of the world and all that is in it. He has already judged Satan and reserved a place for him in the lake of fire according to the Bible in the book of The Revelation.

The Life Application Bible footnote explains it like this:

> Death and Hell are thrown into the Lake of Fire— when God's judgment is finished. The Lake of Fire is the ultimate destination of everything wicked— Satan, the Creature, the False Prophet, the demons. Death, Hell and all those whose names are not recorded in the Book of Life because they have not placed their faith in Jesus Christ.
>
> —RV 20:14, *Life Application Bible: The Living Bible*, page 2000, Tyndale, 1988

## Truth by the Holy Spirit

The Holy Spirit will lead us into all truth in order that we might escape judgment. When we decide we want to follow God's way in everything we do, the Holy Spirit will help us. But we must yield our will to His will. We must want what God wants for our lives and for the world.

> "When the Holy Spirit, who is truth, comes, he shall guide you into all truth, for he will not be presenting his own ideas, but he'll be passing on to you what he has heard."
>
> —John 16: 13a TLB

*Dear God,*

*I need your Holy Spirit in my life. I want to believe in you, no matter what. I want to see your goodness in the earth and I want to escape the judgment that is waiting for all who have not placed their faith in you.*

*I yield my life to your Holy Spirit that I may know truth.*

*(Write your own prayer.)*

Date: _____

Day 22

# Otherside: Our Serving Side

The serving side is developed when we partner with God on earth to bring His goodness or righteousness or to serve God's goodness and righteousness to others. It means we work for God. We are His representative to others.

## God Is Hiring

When we go to work for someone, first they must invite us to interview. During the interview process, we discover what the job requires. If they offer a job, we have the option to accept it or not. The same is true of God. He invites everyone to work for Him but just like in the interview process, not everyone accepts. But when we do accept, we must act appropriately. There are guidelines for any job. We don't just show up and do what we want to do. We are trained and then we do what's required.

The Bible says, "For many are invited but few are chosen" (Matt. 22:14, NIV). That verse implies it's an honor to work for God on the earth. He sends an invitation to many but only a few accept. Those who go through the training and act appropriately are the chosen. Proper behavior is evidence of being chosen.

## God's Training

After accepting the invitation, we must go through the training. This is the learning process whereby we change our way of thinking to agree with God on His goodness and righteousness.

> Don't copy the behavior and customs of this world, but be a new and different person with a fresh newness in all you do and think. Then you will learn from your own experience how his ways will really satisfy you.
>
> —Romans 12:2 TLB

There is a difference between believing in God and heaven and "being chosen" to represent God in the earth. I may believe a diet will help me control my weight, but unless I choose to behave differently, my belief alone won't change anything. It's the action behind something that makes it a reality in our lives.

## Training to Serve

The first step in training to serve with God on earth is to submit to and obey God. Neither of those words is popular in current society. It implies we are less than adequate. Our society demands perfection and self-sufficiency in all areas. Less than perfect is ruining our lives. It's a constant reminder that we are not good enough.

To submit means to yield or surrender our will to God. To obey God means to carry out or to comply with His instructions. When we serve God on earth, we find out what His will is and then we will carry it out.

If we fail to know God's will or carry it out, we essentially don't live under God's authority. We live under our own authority, the authority of another person, or the authority of cultural standards. That means we will submit to and obey our own will, the will of another person, or the will of current culture.

## Who Will You Serve?

Whether we serve God, ourselves, others, or society, the choice is ours. We have the freedom to choose. God made us that way. He needs free agents to represent His kingdom on earth. We all have different personalities and talents so that His kingdom ways can saturate the world.

God doesn't dictate behavior but character. People dictate behavior. But when we allow God to form His character in us, then we will behave accordingly. God's character is formed in us when we submit to and obey God. Then we can use the personality and talents we have to spread the message of His kingdom in the earth. That's how we partner with God on earth.

*Thought provoking questions:*
**Who do you submit to and obey? Whose authority is driving your behavior?**

*Day 23*

## Otherside: Hollywood Says

Serving others is demeaning. It implies forced labor. The media is filled with examples of those forced to serve harsh taskmasters. It's in the news, the movies, television, and games. Only the strong survive is the message.

But what about those whose hearts are tender? Hollywood considers them weak and failing. Society pushes them aside. Sometimes their weaknesses are given a label, permitting an excuse for not measuring up to impossible standards. Or those weaknesses can lead to addictions as a means of escaping society's demands.

### Hollywood's Choices

Hollywood productions present many examples of strength and weakness. There are characters who dominate and those who are dominated by others. We often see ourselves in them.

The choice Hollywood presents is either to be strong or to be weak.

1. Be strong. Dominate. Be powerful. Be in charge. Control. Be influential. Master. Ruler.

    Exerting your own authority over others is exhausting. It also causes you to become insensitive to others because, in society, sensitivity implies weakness. And to dominate, you must appear strong.

    Who hasn't known a bully? Domination is the source of bullying. Domination is an ego out of control. Warning: Forcing someone to recognize your authority has serious consequences. The law gets involved, protecting citizens from bullies. Society recognizes the danger it causes to individuals.

We see bullying in our families, friends, in the streets, in school, and in business. When another person forces their will on you, either physically or verbally, it is wrong. If you are being forced against your will, either get out of the situation or report it to an authority.

2. Be weak. Submit. Incompetent. Frail. Powerless. Hopeless. Inadequate. Inefficient. Inferior.

None of us are complete on our own. None of us are perfect. We all have weaknesses. But not all personalities admit weaknesses. To admit to weakness is humility. Humility is the opposite of pride and arrogance.

Hollywood portrays weak people as lacking in something; physical strength, firmness of character, mental ability, power, resolve, intelligence, persuasiveness, skill, aptitude, and the ability to function normally. Who hasn't felt weak or lacking in something?

## Great Movies

Many great movies are the story of a bully, defeated by an unlikely hero who overcomes a weakness. We love those movies because they give hope and inspiration to overcome our own weaknesses.

Somewhere deep inside, we all desire to have strength. We imagine ourselves as heroines who can take on a bully and subdue the bully with love, breaking the spell, turning life into something wonderful.

> *Can you think of a movie with this theme?*

We believe that love can conquer all. Right? Even in real life, sometimes we are drawn to the bad boy and secretly hope our love will be enough to change him. We have hope in love.

## Beauty and the Beast

The story opens with a prince who is repulsed by the appearance of an old woman asking for help. As he sends her away, she places a spell on him, turning him into an ugly beast. The spell won't be broken until he learns to love another and receives love in return. In reality, we can all become beasts if we can't give and receive love.

Belle, the heroine has weaknesses. Others view her as odd because of her love for books. Her father loves her and desires for her to have the life she wants far away from the village. He gets into trouble trying to meet her needs. Many of us do the same when we try to meet the needs of others and disregard our own safety.

Gaston, a hunter, attempts to dominate Belle into marrying him. He is the despicable guy everyone loves to hate. He is a typical egomaniac that everyone steers clear of. His behavior is blatantly self-serving. He thinks only of himself and what he wants.

Belle becomes strong as she sacrifices her life to take her father's place, whom the Beast is holding captive in the dungeon. Her reward is plenty of books to read in the Beast's library. Belle and the Beast begin a relationship with each other as they show care and concern. This is how relationships begin. And it will grow when the care is returned.

Gaston and the Beast battle to the death. This may be representative of the fight that takes place in each of us as we care for others. Gaston is self-serving and the Beast, who was also self-serving in the beginning, has started to develop caring feelings for Belle. For certain, one or the other will die in our lives—love of self or love for others.

Belle's love saves the Beast at the last moment and the spell is broken. Of course, they live happily ever after.

## The Reality of Love

> …let us continue to love each other since love comes from God.
> Everyone who loves is born of God and experiences a relationship with God.
> The person who refuses to love doesn't know the first thing about God,
> because God is love—so you can't know him if you don't love.
>
> —1Jn 4: 7–8 MSG

According to these verses, you can only truly show love to others when you are experiencing a relationship with God. Any other love is self-serving. Without God, the only reason someone would show care and concern to others is because it might benefit them in some way.

It is easy to be fooled by those who appear to be doing good things. But is their love genuine? Is it a love not motivated by gain? Because that is pure love. That's the God kind of love. That's the kind of love it takes to develop a *Servingside*. When we can learn to give the same kind of care and concern to others that God gives to us, then we have developed our Servingside.

*Lord God,*

*I want to learn to serve others. I want to work for you on the earth to bring your love to others. Help me to not be motivated by what I can get out of a situation. Help me develop a pure love.*

*(Write your own prayer.)*

Date: _____

Day 24

## Otherside: Heaven Says

At the core of Christianity is a call to love others. When we truly love God, our behavior will change. We will want to share God's love with others. We will be able to take our thoughts off ourselves and getting our needs and wants met. We will trust God and be thankful for His provisions. And we will want to work for God and serve others His goodness and righteousness.

"Hey, I've got a new job with a great company."

"What's the job?"

"I'm going to be a goodwill ambassador."

"What's that mean?"

"Well, I am supposed to tell people about the company and all its benefits. And they told me to recruit others, too."

"Are you recruiting me?"

"Maybe."

"Tell me more about it then. What do they sell?"

"A better life."

"A better life? How do they sell a better life? Like more money, new wardrobe, or a place on the beach?"

"No, it's not like that. It's really kinda different. It sort of operates like a pay it forward idea. I'm supposed to recruit by serving others."

"Serving them what?"

"Well, uh, like uh, peace, and uh, kindness, patience… and stuff like that."

"Patience? You gotta be kidding me. Nobody's patient. It almost doesn't exist."

"That's the reason people need to be given patience. The idea is that it's nice to receive patience so hopefully they will give patience to someone in return. You know, pay it forward."

"Yeah, no…I can't see that working."

"And there's more. There are nine things that make a better life."

"So…what are they?

"Love, joy, peace, patience, kindness, gentleness, goodness, faithfulness, and self-control."

"Wow! No losing your temper, shouting, and getting pushy to get your way?"

"Yep, that's right."

"Hmmm."

"I've been told that I may not see it work on the first try, but I just need to keep giving it out to people and I'll see results. It's like the other sales jobs I've had. People usually turn you down the first time, but eventually if you keep at it, you'll see results."

"So how do you get paid?"

"That's the part you might not understand."

"Are you kidding? I already don't understand."

"I get paid in a better life…forever"

"How are you gonna pay the rent with that?"

"I still have to keep my day job. That's how."

"So what's the benefit? Sounds like a lotta work for nothing."

"Less stress. Believe it or not, it takes a whole lot more energy to get mad about something than to be nice about it. And usually you getter better results."

"Yeah, you're probably right."

"And get this, the owner of the company trains everyone. That way, he's sure everyone is doing things like they should be. He gives you a little reminder buzzer to wear on a chain around your neck. It's in the shape of a heart. It stings a little when you're not doing things like you should be."

"Ouch."

"Oh, it doesn't really hurt. It's just a little buzz, like a little shock or something."

"Well, he must be a busy guy if he does all of the training. What's it like, you know, the training?"

"He demonstrates all nine of those things to me."

"How does he do that?"

"Well, I have a book with stories about others he has taught. It tells what and how they learned because everyone learns the same things…but differently. Every day, I read the book and talk to him. He points out things to me in my everyday life. You know, in my own situations."

"How does he point it out?"

"It's like he becomes this invisible friend through the necklace. It reminds to hold my tongue when I want to swear at someone or when I want to lay on my horn in traffic, or cheat my boss out of time. You know, stuff like that."

"Do you have to wear that necklace?"

"As long as I'm working for him, I do. Otherwise, I would just do what I want to do and not what he wants me to do. It's really effective."

"I bet. So…how do you get promoted?"

"He turns you over to his son for more training. You're supposed to follow him as an example of how things are done. And after that, you get in a group of other people so you can practice. Then he turns you loose to show anyone and everyone how to have a better life."

"That's some plan."

"So do you want to join us?"

"What do I have to do?"

"Just say yes."

"That's it?"

"Yep, then he shows up to show you the way to a better life. Then you start learning just like I explained."

"I guess I don't have anything to lose except my temper."

"And all your other bad habits that are keeping you from having a better life."

"Hey, now, wait a sec."

"Yeah, sorry. I'm forgetting. It's pay it forward time. Did I ever tell you what a great friend you are and how lucky I am to know you?"

"Okay, I get it. Now I'm supposed to say what a great friend you are to me, too."

"Only if you really mean it."

"I do."

"Hey, I think it's working. I'm having a better life already!"

When the Holy Spirit comes alive in us, it empowers us to do God's will on earth. Just like the necklace, the Holy Spirit will remind us when we are going the wrong way. We will feel conviction in our hearts. Then we have the opportunity to make things right.

Great things can be accomplished when Christians decide to make a habit of doing God's will on earth. But it usually happens one life at a time and one act of kindness at a time as we pay it forward. As we grow in maturity, God increases our responsibilities.

The more we get to know God, the easier it is to know His will. When we know His will, it will be easier to carry it out.

Day 25

# Your Otherside

Our Otherside, or our servingside, can only be developed when we have a trusting relationship with God. Relationship implies that we are connected to God as if we are related. It's more than casual. It's more than just knowing about Him. It's personal. And it's mutual. He loved us first, now we can love Him back.

> Jesus said, "Love the Lord your God with all of your heart,
> all of your soul, and with all of your mind.
> This is the first and greatest commandment.
> And the second is like it, 'Love your neighbor as yourself.'"
>
> —Mt. 22: 37–39 NIV

## Love God

The greatest commandment is to love God. We can't love Him without knowing Him. We may love the idea of God, someone who is in charge of the universe. But to love God as a person, we must know Him and allow Him to shape our character in this mutual relationship. We want to be pleasing to God. In that way, we can also be pleasing to others. That is the way we represent Him to others. So it becomes important to set aside time to spend with God on a regular basis in order to get to know Him. The following are ways to get to know God:

1. Read the Bible. When we do, we become familiar with how He operates in the lives of others through stories. Joining a Bible study can be important to help understand how the Bible was written. But listening for God to speak directly to you as you read helps personalize it.
2. Meditate. This simply means to set aside time to think about God and His ways.
3. Pray. Prayer is talking to God. Individual prayer is important—one on one—with God. It helps us verbalize our questions and concerns.
4. Journal. Writing our thoughts and prayers in journals helps us see growth in our spiritual life. When we look back, we can see how God answered prayers and questions. This will help us trust God.
5. Give thanks. Remembering the good things God has provided keeps us humble, knowing there are things we can't do without Him. It also pleases God when we show appreciation for Him.

## Love Yourself

God made us unique. There is only one of you. Accepting ourselves means we recognize God's creativity. God desires that we all conform to His character but He knows each of us can express His character to a variety of people. That is the reason for our uniqueness, so that we can each reach a different segment of the world.

If we were all the same, there would be people who may never experience God's ways. He needs all of us to develop an Otherside where we serve God's goodness to the world. If we don't accept our individualism, envy or pride will keep us focused on ourselves, not focused on others.

## Love Your Neighbor

This is our Otherside. When we develop a relationship with friends and neighbors, it opens a door for us to share God's character with them.

Even though we may have a purpose for the relationship, whether it is business or casual, we are obligated to God to share His character with everyone we come in contact with. That is how we share God with the world. That is how we develop our Otherside.

*Dear God,*

*I want to develop my Otherside. I want to show your character to those who desperately need to see you. But I am weak. Help me be strong. Help me know you better. Remind me again what you said to the apostle Paul; that your power is made strong in my weakness. 2 Cor. 12:9*

*I admit my weaknesses to you.*


*Help me love the world like you do.*    Date: _____

# CHALLENGE 3

# Change Your Community

## Why Community?

Did you ever try to accomplish a huge task on your own without any help? If you have, you'll realize you are limited as to what you can do. When we include others who understand the mission, three things happen:

1. More is accomplished.
2. Friendships are formed.
3. Support and encouragement is realized.

## God's Mission

God has a huge mission. His plan is to reconcile humankind to Himself. Simply put that means to reestablish a broken relationship with all of humanity.

In the beginning, humankind walked and talked with God in the garden of paradise. A break in the relationship occurred when Eve and Adam decided to go their own way. Instead of trusting God, they believed the lies of the serpent. They believed they could have something better than a loving relationship with God, living in the garden of paradise where they had a peaceful existence. When they realized what they had done, they had regrets. But they were too ashamed to admit their mistake. Ever since then, God has made it His mission to win our hearts back.

Now, what girl hasn't had regrets of breaking up with a great guy? But she went on with her life. She believed she blew it and believed there was no way to reconcile the relationship. So she kept looking for someone to take his place. What if that great guy really loved her and enlisted the help of his friends to show her how much he loved her? If that were you, would you stay away in shame and regret or would you run into his open arms of forgiveness?

It's the same with God. He loves us so much that he will stop at nothing to get us back. He hopes that we return to a relationship with Him. God knows it's a huge undertaking to reconcile the relationship He once had with humankind. So He has enlisted the help of others throughout history to tell humankind how much He loves us and forgives us for the breakup. God has made friends with people throughout history. As friends are added, they all share common stories of how they came into a relationship with God. That's how God's community began and continues to grow.

## God's Community Accomplishes More

A community is a group of people who have a common interest; they share, participate, and fellowship together under the same government or ruling philosophy. For some, the word government implies strict rules, regulations, and enforcement. Although God's community has a government, it operates more by a ruling philosophy or core truth.

The core truth of God's community is that He wants to be reconciled with humankind, or to be in relationship with each person. That is the core truth that forms His community. God's community is known as the Church.

God can accomplish this huge task—reconciling His relationship with humankind—when more people become involved. Becoming a part of a local church is the way to become a part of that community. It's a group of people who have God's interests as their common interests. We learn, share, participate and fellowship under the core truth of God's love for humankind.

## In God's Community, Friendships Form

When we spend time together, friendships will form. It happens in families, schools, and businesses. God made us relational. In other words, we are drawn together out of a common interest. That common interest may be because of family ties, school or business associates, hobbies, or other groups who share similarities. Our interests draw us together and friendships form.

In God's community, we are drawn together because of God's interests, not necessarily because of our own interests. In the Bible, we are told, "We love him, because he first loved us" (1 Jn. 4:19,

NIV). God draws us into His circle. Then we find our interests in this community of believers. We form a friendship with God first, then we learn to share our experience with others that God has drawn in or those who he is currently drawing into relationship with Him.

We may not be like the others in our community. We may not share any other interests with them, but we are in a relationship with them. God refers to the Church as His bride, His body, and His family. All those terms indicate an intimate relationship He has with a group of people based on His love for us all.

Those who enter into a relationship with God also enter into a relationship with others who have been reconciled to God. We share the same Father, Son, and Holy Spirit. It's as if we're working for the family business now and the boss is the Father. We each have a responsibility to the Father to see that His mission is accomplished. We all have a different part to play and it's important to respect others who play a different part than you. It would be boring if we were all the same. God made variety for a purpose. You may find, out of respect, friendships will form.

## Support and Encouragement in Community

Respecting someone means we are willing to show consideration and appreciation for them. We take the time to think about their circumstances before forming an opinion. When we immediately form an opinion without considering their circumstances, then we judge them by our own opinion.

Realizing that others in God's community are not perfect puts us all in the same boat. None of us are perfect. But we all are trying to accomplish the same goal—to be in a relationship with God and to encourage others in His community who are trying to do the same.

That's where we need to give and get support and encouragement. To support implies strength. When others in our community become weak or begin to slip, we should support them with encouragement. To inspire others with hope, courage, and confidence is our duty in our community. God doesn't want to lose any of us again.

When others in our community are weak, speaking words of encouragement will help reinforce the fact that God loves them, forgives them, and wants to spend eternity with them. And when we are willing to support and encourage them, they will likely do the same for us in times of our weakness. That's how God's community works.

## Growing Up in Our Community

Babies are self-centered. They cry when they need or want something. They are unaware of the world around them. They don't even know they are a part of a family. They only know they exist. As children grow, they learn how to interact with others. They learn they are a part of something bigger. First a family, then a neighborhood, then school, then a community. They learn to realize the needs of others and react accordingly. That is called maturing.

God wants His followers to be in a community with others and to realize others' needs as well as our own. A part of being in God's community is to learn maturity. We are all connected to God by His Holy Spirit. We have the same spiritual DNA, but we all express ourselves differently. Like brothers and sisters from the same family, we have similarities and differences. But as we mature, each of us has a part to play in the community of God.

*Read: Ephesians 4: 3–5, 11–16*
*This is what I learned from reading this passage from the Bible:*

*This is my prayer about what I've learned:*

Day 27

## Who Is My Community?

All who are reconciled to God by being in relationship with Him (not simply believe in Him) are a part of His bride, His body, and His family. This is the collective community of believers in God. Many ask why there are so many churches if all believe the same core truth. There are a variety of personalities and objectives. We each have a soul where our preferences live. We are drawn to what we like. Churches, like humans, express themselves differently.

    The main consideration about your choice of church is whether they speak the truth of the Bible. Churches are made up of people so they battle living according to cultural standards rather than God's standards just like we do. But if those cultural standards are the basis of the church, we had better beware. Peter and John, Jesus's disciples, wrote letters and included warnings to Christians about false teachers. It is still true of today.

> "…there will be false teachers among you. They will cleverly tell their lies about God… Many will follow their evil teaching that there is nothing wrong with sexual sin. And because of them Christ and his way will be scoffed at."
>
> —2 Peter 2: 1a–2 TLB
>
> "…don't always believe everything you hear just because someone says it is a message from God: test it first to see if it really is. For there are many false teachers around, and the way to find out if their message is from the Holy Spirit is to ask: Does it really agree that Jesus Christ, God's Son, actually became man with a human body? If so, then the message is from God. If not, the message is not from God but from one who is against Christ, like the "Antichrist" you have heard about

> who is going to come, and his attitude of enmity against Christ is already abroad in the world.
>
> Dear young friends, you belong to God and have already won your fight with those who are against Christ, because there is someone in your hearts who is stronger than any evil teacher in this wicked world. These men belong to this world, so, quite naturally, they are concerned about worldly affairs and the world pays attention to them. But we are children of God; that is why only those who have walked and talked with God will listen to us."
>
> —1 John 4: 1–6a TLB

Having your own relationship with God and knowing what the Bible says will help guard against those lies.

## My Part in the Community

When we decide to accept God's forgiveness and enter into a relationship with Him, we will have a part to play in our community. God has given gifts and talents to everyone. We also each have a calling or something we feel we were meant to do. This often has to do with the gifts or talents that we are born with or that we have developed out of an interest or natural inclination. Those gifts and calling can be used to benefit the community of God. We will want to become part of a local church where our gifts and callings can be utilized because God needs each of us to accomplish something with what he has given us.

> "Now God gives us many kinds of special abilities, but it is the same Holy Spirit who is the source of them all. There are different kinds of service to God, but it is the same Lord we are serving. There are many ways in which God works in our lives, but it is the same God who does the work in and through all of us who are his. The Holy Spirit displays God's power through each of us as a means of helping the church."
>
> —1 Cor. 12: 4–7 TLB

Just as there are towns, cities, and states in America, there are small, medium, and large churches. When choosing a church, the idea is to become involved with helping God in His mission to reconcile humankind to Him. We don't just belong to a church like it's a social club. We all have something to do, helping in God's mission.

> "To one person the Spirit gives the ability to give wise advice; someone else may be especially good at studying and teaching, and this is his gift from the same Spirit. He gives special faith to another, and someone else the power to heal the sick. He gives power for doing miracles to some, and to others power to prophesy and preach. He gives someone else the power to know whether evil spirits are speaking through those who claim to be giving God's message – or whether it is really the Spirit of God who is speaking. Still another person is able to speak in languages he never learned; and others, who do not know the language either, are given power to understand what he is saying. It is the same and only Holy Spirit who gives all these gifts and power, deciding which each one us should have.
>
> —1 Cor. 12:8–11 TLB

Note: Take the online free Spiritual Gifts Analysis, Church Growth Institute.org.

## One Calling for All

Many feel inadequate to help God in His mission so they hold back. While it's true, we all should make sure our personal relationship with God is in good standing, our mission is also to help others reconcile to God. We can use our testimony, or the things we've been through and learned as an encouragement to others. We don't have to be perfect to help God with His mission, but we should continue to pursue and develop our personal relationship with God as we serve others through the church.

There is one thing we all are capable of to help God in His mission. That one thing is to love others. That is how we share God with others. We are all capable of it in our relationships, with God's help. When we experience God's love and forgiveness first, then we will be able to do the same for others. 1 Corinthians 13 is part of a letter the apostle Paul wrote to a community of believers in the city of Corinth. He encouraged them to love each other in this way.

> He begins by saying, "…let me tell you about something else that is better than any of [the gifts of the Holy Spirit]"
>
> —1 Cor. 12:31b LB
>
> "All the special gifts and powers from God will someday come to an end, but love goes on forever."
>
> —1 Cor. 13: 8a LB
>
> "Love is very patient and kind, never jealous or envious, never boastful or proud, never haughty or selfish or rude. Love does not demand its own way. It is not irritable or touchy. It does not hold grudges and will hardly even notice when others do it wrong. It is never glad about injustice, but rejoices whenever truth wins out. If you love someone you will be loyal to him no matter what the cost. You will always believe in him, always expect the best of him, and always stand your ground in defending him."
>
> —1Cor. 13: 4–7 LB

These verses from the Bible are used often in wedding ceremonies as an example of how we should act in marriage. And these words are a good charge for couples. For if we don't learn how to love in an intimate relationship with a husband, then how can we love others in God's community or in the world?

How can we accept God's love and learn to love others? By believing what the Bible says. The chart below shows we are loved by God; we can be secure in God's love for us; and we are significant because of God's love. When we believe these verses, then we can put them into action in our lives as we reach out to others in our community. As we are encouraged by reading them, we can encourage others in words and deeds. Then we can serve others with our gifts and talents and a pure heart. Otherwise, without love for others, we will only serve ourselves with our gifts and talents. Our motives won't be pure. They will be for personal gain and fame. When we truly love others, our gifts and talents will be a blessing to them.

## You Are Accepted, Secure, and Significant in God's Community

I Am Accepted:

I am God's Child John 1:12
I am Christ's friend John 15:15
I have been justified Roman 5:1
I am united with the Lord and I am one Spirit with him 1 Cor. 6:17
I have been bought with a price. I belong to God. 1 Cor. 6:20
I am a member of Christ's body 1 Cor. 12:27
I have been adopted as God's child. Eph. 1:5
I have direct access to God through the Holy Spirit. Eph. 2:18
I have been redeemed and forgiven of all my sins. Col. 1:13, 14

## I Am Secure

I am free from condemnation. Rom. 8: 1, 2
I am assured that all things work together for good. Rom. 8:28
I am free from any condemning charges against me. Rom. 8: 31–34
I have been established, anointed and sealed by God. 2 Cor. 1: 21, 22
I am confident that the good work God has begun in me
    will be completed. Phl. 1:6
I am a citizen of Heaven. Phl. 3:20
I have not been given a spirit of fear, but of power,
    love and self-discipline. 2 Tim. 1:7
I can find grace and mercy in time of need. Heb. 4:16
I am born of God and the evil one cannot touch me. 1 Jn. 5:18

## I Am Significant

I am the salt and light of the earth. Mt. 5: 13, 14
I am a branch of the true vine, a channel of his life. John 15, 1, 5
I have been chosen and appointed to bear fruit. John 15: 16
I am a personal witness of Christ. Acts 1: 8
I am God's temple. 1 Cor. 5: 17–21
I am a minister of reconciliation for God. 2 Cor. 5: 17–21
I am God's co-worker. 2 Cor. 6: 1 (1 Co. 3:9)
I am seated with Christ in the Heavenly Realm. Eph. 2: 6
I am God's workmanship. Eph. 2:10

*Dear God,*

*I want to use my gifts and talents to help you in your mission to the world. But first, I want to learn to love. Teach me to love. I need to know you love me. As I experience your love then I believe I will be able to show love to others.*

*(Write your own prayer)*

Day 28

## Heaven's Community

We all need a place to belong, to know that we are a part of something bigger. That something bigger is church when we become Christians. The church is a place where we learn about faith, practice faith, and are encouraged in our faith. It's where and how we learn to put heaven's principles into action.

Many have a misconception about church. They think the pastor does all the work. They come to a banquet every week that has been prepared and served. While it's true the pastor plays a key role in most churches, there are many other responsibilities in your community. Your community needs your gifts and talents. You are important, no matter how small you think your part is. Paul of the Bible described it like this in a letter to the church at Corinth.

> "The body is a unit, though it is made up of many parts; and though all its parts are many, they form one body. So it is with Christ. For we were all baptized by one Spirit into one body—whether Jews or Greeks, slave or free—and we were all given the one Spirit to drink. Now the body is not made up of one part but of many. If the foot should say, "Because I am not a hand, I do not belong to the body," it would not for that reason cease to be part of the body. And if the ear should say, "Because I am not an eye, I do not belong to the body," it would not for that reason cease to be part of the body. If the whole body were an eye, where would the sense of hearing be? If the whole body were an ear, where would the sense of smell be? But in fact God has arranged the parts in the body, every one of them, just as he wanted them to be. If they were all one part, where would the body be? As it is, there are many parts, but one body. The eye cannot say to the hand, "I don't need you!" And the head cannot say to the feet, "I don't need you!" On the contrary, those parts of the body that seem to be weaker are indispensable, and the parts that we think are less honorable we treat with special honor. And the parts that are unpresentable are treated with special modesty, while our presentable parts need no special treatment. But God has combined the members of the body and has given greater honor to the parts that lacked it, so that there should be no division in the body, but that its parts should have equal concern for each other. If one part suffers, every part suffers with it; if one part is honored, every part rejoices with it. Now you are the body of Christ, and each one of you is a part of it.
>
> —1 Corinthians 12: 12–27 NIV

## You Are a Part of God's Community

No matter how insignificant you think you are, your community needs you. Even if you think you are no more important than a big toe, don't underestimate its importance. The big toe gives balance for the entire body. Just as nothing in our body is insignificant, no one in God's community is insignificant. He needs each of us.

As we grow in our relationship with God and become confident of His love, we will naturally want to reach out to others. Reaching out to the world to show God's love can be tough because it is a mean world. That's why we have community. We learn of God's love and practice giving that same kind of love to others when we have a community of believers to share with. That confidence helps us reach out to the world.

## God's Plan for His Community

God's plan from the beginning was to live in harmony with humankind. But humankind chose to separate from God and build a world of their own, doing things their own way. It was very difficult, if not impossible to do without God.

In His love for humanity, He came into this world as Jesus the man. Jesus became the example, showing us how to enter back into a relationship with God. He lived differently than others, even performing miracles to prove Himself. His biggest miracle, defying death as He came to life after He died, got everyone's attention. And it still has people talking.

Communities of those who believed what Jesus taught while He was on earth began to form. They encouraged each other to enter into a relationship with God through accepting His Holy Spirit into their lives. Because of their enthusiasm, the message of reconciliation to God continues to spread to this day.

There will be a day when all who are reconciled to God will live in community with one another. That community is the coming Heaven. It is promised throughout the Bible. No one knows when that time will come or exactly how it will occur. But because we believe the history of the Bible, what has already passed, we believe in the future that the Bible tells of.

## God's Plan for You in His Community

In the meantime, our purpose is to enter into a relationship with God through His Holy Spirit. We do this by saying yes to God in our hearts. The way we have a relationship is to talk to God in prayer, and give time and attention to thinking about God's ways as they are written in the Bible. Then we apply those things to our lives. That is how our forever destiny of Heaven is sure.

> Jesus said…"Not everyone who says to me, 'Lord, Lord, will enter the kingdom of heaven, but only he who does the will of my Father who is in heaven."
>
> —Matthew 7: 21 NIV

Learning to do the will of God is a part of living in community. If we will spend eternity with others who are believers, shouldn't we start learning to do that now? That's a part of joining others in church. It teaches us how to love others.

> Here's how we can be sure that we know God in the right way; Keep his commandments.
> If someone claims, "I know him well!" but doesn't keep his commandments, he's obviously a liar. His life doesn't match his words. But the one who keeps God's word is the person in whom we see God's mature love. This is the only way to be sure we're in God. Anyone who claims to be intimate with God ought to live the same kind of life Jesus lived."
>
> —I John 2: 3–6 MSG

*Dear God*

*Please show me that I belong to your community, both now and forever. Help me to know and to do your will.*

*(Write your own prayer.)*

*Date: _____*

Day 29

# Maintaining Your New Reality

## The Big Picture Show

This Hollywood world is all about pretend and make-believe, but we continue to adjust our lives according to its standards because of the influence it has on us. It's all show, pretense, and artificial. It does not represent the lives we are instructed to live as followers of Christ.

## The Big Picture

God has a big picture in mind, but we can't grasp it because it's too big for us. His plan is our purpose. Our purpose begins with trust that God has a bigger picture in mind, and He has all things under His control. This is everything God wants for us:

1. Learn to love God
2. Learn to love others

This is the sum of our Christian life. It seems so simple but it is truly difficult, and we will spend a lifetime accomplishing it.

We have learned we are made in God's image as triune beings—Skinside (body), Inside (soul), and Deeperside (spirit)—and we have qualities that cause us to be unique. This allows Christians to be in a variety of situations whereby we can demonstrate His qualities to those around us through our Otherside (serving). God wants us to show the world His character in whatever circumstance or situation we find ourselves. This is how we influence the world for God. Jesus instructed us this way so that the world might have hope because of us. Our mission is to be different than this world. We don't have to look far for the opportunity to show God's character to those around us.

- Family
- Church members
- Friends
- Neighbors
- Coworkers
- Volunteer groups
- Those who serve us

## Spend Time with God

Unless we spend time with God, we won't know Him or His character. We may know about Him by hearing what others have to say about Him, but we won't know Him intimately or personally. We must commit time with Him in order to know Him. When we get to know Him, He will speak to our hearts in our deepest needs or direct us in our circumstances. Then we will know He loves us and is concerned about the things that concern us. Ask God to make Himself known to you in an intimate way.

> "Keep on asking, and you will receive what you ask for. Keep on seeking, and you will find. Keep on knocking, and the door will be opened to you.
>
> For everyone who asks, receives. Everyone who seeks, finds. And to everyone who knocks, the door will be opened.
>
> "You parents—if your children ask for a loaf of bread, do you give them a stone instead?
>
> Or if they ask for a fish, do you give them a snake? Of course not!
>
> So if you sinful people know how to give good gifts to your children, how much more will your heavenly Father give good gifts to those who ask him.
>
> —Matthew 7: 7–11 NLB

## Made for God's Purpose

When we read the Bible, pray, and journal, we are getting to know God and the love He has for us. When we know His love, we won't be so desperate to settle for substitutes—acceptance from other people. Only when we begin to glimpse the love He has for us can we understand that those around us have needs also. We are called to be God's hand in the earth by and through the help of the Holy Spirit.

## How Can We Stay Heaven Bound in a Hollywood World?

- Keep on affirming your faith to yourself and others
- Accept yourself as God made you and accept the differences in others
- Emphasize your strengths, work on your weakness, and use your God-given gifts in all of your relationships and circumstances
- Live from your Deeperside, in relationship with God, and He will guide you
- Believe God's plan and purpose for each of us is giving hope in a hopeless world with whatever gifts, talents, and calling you have
- Live your life as a Christian, not simply believing in God, but by knowing Him and partnering with Him, making the world a better place.

Day 30

# Warning: Beware of Identity Theft

Once you commit your life to following God, you will be tempted to return to your old ways. After all, those ways were the habits of your life and you will need to retrain your habits. They say it takes 30 days to break or begin a new habit. This is the 30th day of your journey to change your world so you are on your way to a new beginning.

## The Thief Who Steals

God has had an enemy since the beginning of the Bible. He was referred to as the serpent in the story of Eve and Adam. He is also referred to as Satan, the devil, Lucifer, the evil one, the angel of light, and the prince of this world. Basically, he's the bad guy. He tries to get us to follow him and His ways over God and God's ways. It's kind of like we're caught up in this heavenly battle, playing tug of war. God pulls on our hearts; Satan pulls on our heads, as he causes us to rationalize and justify living our lives in order to please ourselves.

God understands the tug of war we are in. He's been battling this enemy for a long time and he knows how sneaky Satan is. God makes provision for us in the form of forgiveness. In other words, when we fail God and follow Satan, God is always faithful to receive us back into a relationship with Him. But He hopes we learn our lesson. He hopes we won't fall for the tricks of Satan the next time he tempts us.

## How the Thief Steals

The nature of humankind is to be concerned about our natural circumstances, or what we experience with our five senses in this world. But the spiritual nature that comes by living from our Deeperside is to see with our spiritual eyes into a world that is not yet visible.

Jesus came from the invisible world to the visible world and returned to the invisible world. He promised heaven (the invisible world) to those who would believe. Jesus's message while He was on earth was about The Kingdom of Heaven. Jesus said we should bring that kingdom to earth. The way we do that is by first believing then acting on what we believe. His prayer was that we could live like citizens of that kingdom while we are here on earth.

But the earth is the battleground on which we fight to live like citizens of heaven. Even Jesus experienced temptation after He was baptized. You can read His story in Matthew 4:1–10. So if Jesus experienced temptation and He is our example, we will experience it too. Below are three battlegrounds we will fight on.

- The flesh
- The devil
- The world

**The Flesh: Our Human Nature**

The flesh, or our natural inclinations as humankind, is a battleground. Human nature desires convenience, comfort, and pleasure. But that isn't always God's plan. Sometimes when our desires of convenience, comfort, and pleasure aren't met, then we turn to God. It causes us to realize how much we need God. But sometimes, rather than trust God, we are tempted to try to meet our own needs.

Jesus was tempted in the flesh, too, or by His natural desires. After He was baptized, He was led out into the desert in order to fast for forty days and to overcome His human desire. He was hungry after fasting.

> After fasting forty days and forty nights, he was hungry. The tempter came to him and said, "If you are the Son of God, tell these stones to become bread."
>
> Jesus answered, "It is written; 'Man does not live on bread alone, but on every word that comes from the mouth of God,'"
>
> —Matthew 4: 2–4 NIV

*I am tempted by my own human nature with:*

*I want to trust God with:*

## The Devil: Our Doubts

Another battleground is doubt. God's enemy will use doubt to cause us to disbelieve God, the Bible, and the promises of heaven. Satan will cause us to be uncertain of God's love, forgiveness, and purpose. After all, the things of God are invisible and it's much easier to trust things we can experience with our five senses. Those things are real while we live in our bodies, but they won't last throughout eternity. The things of this world will go away and God's kingdom will emerge. Don't let Satan steal the promises of God with doubt.

Jesus was tempted to doubt God also, but He handled it with His faith. He called upon God by quoting verses from the Old Testament laws written in the book of Deuteronomy.

> Then the devil took him to the holy city and had him stand on the highest point of the temple. "If you are the Son of God," he said, "throw yourself down. For it is written:
>
> "He will command his angels concerning you, and they will lift you up in their hands, so that you will not strike your foot against a stone."
>
> Jesus answered him, "It is also written: 'Do not put the Lord your God to the test.'"
>
> —Matthew 4: 5–7 NIV

*I am tempted to doubt when:*

*I want to believe God loves me, forgives me, and that my life has purpose:*

### The World: Our Desires for Material Things

Material possessions are a great battleground. We have addressed the expectations of the Hollywood world we live in. All around us are deceptive images of who we should become and what we should have in this life. It's difficult to shield ourselves against its messages. But one way is to learn who God says we are and to put our attention on a heavenly world. Remember your goal of being heaven bound.

Satan tempted Jesus with material things also. He tempted Jesus with wealth and power if Jesus would only worship him.

> Again, the devil took him to a very high mountain and showed him all the kingdoms of the world and their splendor. "All this I will give you,' he said, "if you will bow down and worship me."
>
> Jesus said to him, "Away from me, Satan! For it is written; 'Worship the Lord your God, and serve him only.'
>
> —Matthew 4: 8–10 NIV

## Status Update

Despite the thief who comes to steal, kill, and destroy, we must determine to follow God and His ways while we are on the earth. It will be a battle that will be worth it.

Jesus said…"The thief's purpose is to steal and kill and destroy. My purpose is to give them a rich and satisfying life."

—John 10: 10 NLT

"No eye has seen, no ear has heard, and no mind has imagined what God has prepared for those who love him."

—1Co 2: 9 NLT

*My Status Update:*

# CHALLENGE 4

## Change Your Story

## Past

Oftentimes, our past keeps us from moving forward. We might have regrets; wishing things could have been different. We continue to be disappointed, mourning the loss of something or someone. We do the replay in our heads, blaming ourselves or someone else for our loss.

In order to move forward in life, it's important to realize those things happened and there is nothing we can do to make it different. And the danger of playing out those various scenes in our head is we set ourselves up for disappointment again. We develop a set of expectations based on a particular set of circumstances that will never happen again.

God has provided a way to move forward and not stay stuck in our past. He knew life would be full of disappointments. He knew other people would always let us down. He knew we would try to play judge and jury according to our expectations and standards when it comes to others. And He knew we would be tempted to let it ruin our lives with not forgiving others, staying stuck with anger, hatred, and bitterness.

## Forgiveness Releases Me

This is one of the major teachings of Christianity. It's about God forgiving us for all that we have done. In the Old Testament times, the Jewish people were required to sacrifice animals for their sins so they could receive forgiveness. Jesus became that sacrifice for our sins. It was a one-time sacrifice for all of humankind, for all of history. That's why we no longer sacrifice animals. Jesus, referred to as the Lamb of God, died on the cross as a sacrifice for us. All we need to do is to believe we are forgiven. And that's the hard part.

But harder than that is what God requires of us in return—that is, to forgive others when they sin, or bring an offense against us. Just like God pardoned us for our offenses against Him, we are asked to pardon others.

> Jesus said it like this: "For if you forgive men when they sin against you, our heavenly Father will also forgive you. But if you do not forgive men their sins, your Father will not forgive your sins."
>
> —Matthew 6: 14 NIV

The way to move on from your past is forgiveness. That means we no longer hold people responsible for the loss we have experienced. We certainly don't forget but when we forgive, we are no longer their judge. God is their judge. We trust God to make things right because there is no way we can make it right.

## Journal Past Your Past

Spend some time thinking about your past. Are there people or situations that continue to steal your thoughts? Is there someone you haven't forgiven? It might even be you. Do you want to receive God's forgiveness in your life? Then release yourself from your past by forgiving. Move forward into the present and the future.

_____
_____
_____
_____
_____
_____
_____
_____

Day 32

# Present

Welcome to the present! I'm glad you've arrived to living in the now. No more letting the past hold you down. You have a new beginning.

That's not to say you won't be influenced by your past. You will be. What has happened is a part of you and your story. That part can't be changed. But what can change is the way you look at your past. Rather than be disappointed, realize God needs every one of us to make a difference in the life of at least one other person. Our past experiences may have prepared us for making a difference in the life of someone else.

> And we know that all that happens to us is working for our good if we love God and are fitting into his plans.
>
> —Romans 8:28 TLB

## A Life of Worship

Worship kind of seems like an old-fashioned word. It is used many times in the Bible. God wants humankind to worship Him. He wants us to adore Him with love and devotion. Seems kind of weird that He would require that kind of relationship with us, but if you study the Bible, you will find that God is jealous of our affections. It is so important that it is the first of the Ten Commandments.

> "I am Jehovah your God who liberated you from your slavery in Egypt. You may worship no other god than me."
>
> —Exodus 20: 2, 3 TLB

God wants our thoughts to be on Him. He knows that's how we will be protected in our thought life. Our mind will lead us to many places, many of which we shouldn't go. But when our mind is on God—His forgiveness, His goodness, and His purposes for our lives—it will help us in the battles of temptation.

Recalling the blessings of our lives and thanking God is a sure way to worship Him. Journaling prayers and answers is another way. Enjoying nature and God's creation is worship for the beauty He put around us.

## Journal Your Present with Worship

Take some time just to think about God and the good things He is doing in your life and in the lives of others you know. Ask Him to fill your present with thoughts that bring Him honor.

_____
_____
_____
_____
_____
_____
_____
_____
_____
_____
_____
_____

# HEAVEN BOUND IN A HOLLYWOOD WORLD

Day 33

# Future

**Abbey's Story**

Abbey celebrated her tenth birthday yesterday. She loved cookies and would often make her own from a roll of dough, wrapped in plastic, that Mom bought at the store. But feeling like a big girl now, she asked Mom if she could make Grandma's cookies, the best cookies on earth, from scratch.

"Sure you can, Abbey. We'll need to get Grandma's recipe and the ingredients from the store."

Abbey called Grandma for the recipe and carefully wrote down the directions. Then she gave a list of ingredients to Mom.

"Abbey, why don't you come to the store with me and you can pick out the ingredients yourself?"

Abbey was excited because Mom usually went to the store alone. She said bringing the kids was a distraction because they wanted everything they saw. Abbey decided she would only ask Mom for the ingredients for the cookies and nothing else.

When they got home, Mom gave Abbey space on the counter for her ingredients. But Abbey wanted to go play with Suzie next door.

"I'll make the cookies later," she said as she ran out the door.

Mom sighed as she put away the groceries and prepared dinner. When Dad came home from work, he noticed the ingredients for the cookies on the counter.

"What's that for?" he asked.

"Abbey wants to make Grandma's cookies so she went to the store with me to get the ingredients. But she wanted to play instead of bake cookies. Maybe she'll make them after dinner."

After dinner, Abbey had homework to do. Then she wanted to watch her favorite show on TV. Before long, it was time for bed.

A week later, the ingredients were still on the counter. Mom decided to leave them out as a reminder to Abbey. Every evening, when dad came home from work, he asked about the cookies. Abbey's response was always an excuse for something else she wanted to do instead. He decided to have a talk with Abbey.

"I thought you wanted to make some cookies?"

"I do, but I didn't think it would be so much work. The cookie dough roll is a lot easier."

"But they're not as good. They're just average. I know you love Grandma's cookies better than anything."

Abbey hung her head.

"Abbey, since you're a big girl now, I think you should learn a big girl lesson. You have all the ingredients for something wonderful just sitting here. But as long as they just sit there, they will never be cookies. It takes effort on your part to make them into something wonderful. It's a little bit like life. You have all the makings of being something wonderful, but unless you put a little effort into making something out of it, well then, you'll be stuck with a cookie dough roll kind of life."

They both laughed. Abbey understood.

"Come on, let's go to the kitchen. I'll help you."

Dad explained it well. Nothing above average, wonderful, or excellent just happens even though you might have all the right stuff. It takes effort.

God's hope is that we have above average, wonderful, and excellent lives. He has provided all the ingredients we need and a community to support and encourage us toward it. Just like Grandma's cookies as the prize, we have heaven as our prize. But heaven comes with some effort. God promises to help us in that effort.

## Journal Your Future

Christians who follow God in all His ways can be certain of heaven as our destination. But the future of life on earth is uncertain. When we ask God to be the center of our life, He will guide us in our choices. We can trust Him with our dreams, hopes, and goals. God wants us to succeed and be an influence for Him on earth.

Spend some time thinking about your future. God wants to be the center of your everything, but He wants your dreams, hopes, and goals fulfilled, too. He teaches us through our circumstances and shows us His love in tangible ways. What are your thoughts and plans for the future?

_____
_____
_____
_____
_____
_____:Date

# Epilogue

Congratulations! You have just completed the 33-day challenge to change your world. Getting a new view of your reality, your identity, and your community will help you change the story of your life.

This is not a formula for a successful life; instead, it's an encouragement to develop your own personal relationship with God through conversations with Him in prayer, and listening for His response in your heart through regular Bible reading as you meditate and journal. When you do this, you will be assured of your identity and purpose.

As your life circumstances change, you may want to revisit this book and update your journal. It will help you realize spiritual growth.

Staying heaven bound in a Hollywood world is an effort that will be worth it.

> Jesus is credited with saying this: Here on earth you will have many trials and sorrows; but cheer up, for I have overcome the world.
>
> —John 16:33, TLB

www.ingramcontent.com/pod-product-compliance
Lightning Source LLC
Chambersburg PA
CBHW081356290426
44110CB00018B/2397